Frontier Military Series
X

Major General John W. Davidson, U.S. Army
From a photograph about 1865

Black Jack Davidson

A CAVALRY COMMANDER
on the
WESTERN FRONTIER

the life of

General John W. Davidson

by
HOMER K. DAVIDSON
Captain U.S. Navy, Retired

THE ARTHUR H. CLARK COMPANY
Glendale, California
1974

Contents

Illustrations

Introduction

During the research of an enormous number of documents, official and unofficial, historical writings, personal letters, newspaper items, and other information pertaining to the opening and settling of the Western United States, one fact became quite clear. One of those who took a prominent part in the action, and contributed much, yet received little credit by historical writers, is General John W. Davidson, U.S. Army. His contemporaries were Ranald Mackenzie, Nelson A. Miles, George A. Custer, and a host of others who received for their exploits a large amount of favorable publicity – no doubt it was deserved. But, there is no disputing the fact that General Davidson's contributions were as great, and in many cases greater than those who were so highly publicized. It is the purpose of this biography, therefore, to give credit where it is long overdue, in as objective a manner as is possible for the grandson of General Davidson to do.

Certainly some readers of this work will wonder how closely I have hewed to the pattern of historical fact. To them I can say, categorically, that the main facts, dates and events are as near exact as painstaking research can make them. There will also be some who question the lack of precise annotation in some parts of this work. Perhaps that is best explained by saying that many of the events, actions, etc. in which General Davidson was involved, were pieced together from bits and scraps of information gleaned from numerous books, letters, news items, and family records. In those instances it would be a physical impossibility to list them all.

Until the outbreak of the Civil War, General Davidson probably received as much favorable notice as most of the other army officers who were serving in equivalent ranks. But, from the time he became a brigadier general in the Army of the Potomac, in early 1862, until the end of his career the favorable notices seemed to diminish more and more as the years rolled by. That lack became particularly noticeable when reaching the period of his operations in the Great Southwest, in those decades immediately following the end of the Civil War. The soldiers on the frontier were, then, deeply involved in efforts to pacify the thousands of hostile Indians who resented, rightly or wrongly, the incursion of the countless whites who were rapidly settling the West. These whites occupied lands that the Indians believed were rightly theirs. Grandfather was one of those soldiers who were designated for the task of making the West a safe place for settlers to live and raise their families. Unfortunately, from a favorable publicity point of view, he got himself assigned to the Tenth Cavalry.

The Tenth was one of the two Negro cavalry regiments that had been authorized by the national administration. They were Negro in the sense that all enlisted personnel were Negro and the officers were white. Although the Tenth was usually commanded by Colonel Benjamin H. Grierson, the second in command, Lieutenant Colonel John W. Davidson, actually commanded that regiment in the field for several years during the 1870s. Once the Negro regiments arrived in the Southwest there was little delay in giving them a "baptism of fire," in which they acquitted themselves with credit. From that time forward the Indian skirmishes, and full-scale wars were almost daily occurrences. As time wore on the Negro troopers performed their tasks with distinction. Yet, until recent years, the pages of history were filled with the accomplishments of the 4th, 5th, 6th, and 7th Cavalry Regiments, which were all white. Not much was written about the Negro troopers in the 9th and 10th Cavalry Regiments. In fact those two units were given little more than passing notice, and often were completely ignored. Fortunately this situation is being corrected by modern writers. But, as I researched the activities of the Tenth Cavalry the message came through loud and clear – the only obstacles those Negro soldiers could not overcome were prejudice and discrimination.

During General Davidson's period of service with the Tenth Cavalry he was branded, by some historical writers, as being fond of army "spit and polish," something that was dear to the hearts of "West Pointers." The connotation being that "spit and polish" and "West Pointer" were somewhat unsavory terms. Little do they realize the disciplinary value of "spit and polish," nor the all-inclusiveness of the term. "Spit and polish" includes readiness, preventive maintenance, and conduct on the battlefield where the undisciplined act of a single individual can jeopardize the lives of many. In short, it is synonomous with an old, well-known, and very pertinent term – "keep your powder dry." From this writer's point of view some of our modern-day military organizations are entirely too lacking in the old "spit and polish" that once made this country a great military power.

Those few authors who criticized General Davidson usually mentioned him in passing, basing their judgements upon documents that are from ninety to one hundred years old. At times he was represented as a petty tyrant, unreasonable, and given to playing favorites. Unfortunately such remarks were based upon incomplete research information, which produced a completely onesided picture. It is obvious that too much reliance was placed upon the writings of the few who did dislike him with a passion. It must be remembered, however, that it is a proven fact that those who fancy themselves as unjustly treated are very vocal, while the ones who are satisfied with their lot have little or nothing to say. The files that are most useful in providing one with an objective analysis of the man are, John W. Davidson's Appointment, Commission and Personal file, and the medical history file, all of which are in the National Archives. In fairness to all, the state of General Davidson's health was, at times, such that any gentlemanly officer would become irascible or peevish while so affected. Also in fairness to many historians, they made every effort to represent him as strict but fair. This writer believes that to be true.

One of the interesting facts about the Tenth Cavalry, which was characteristic of many regiments in the Southwest, is that it was a rare instance when the entire regiment came together in one location. As a general rule the companies of a regiment were stationed, in groups of two to four, in several different forts. Therefore a regimental commander seldom saw all of his subordinate officers. Generally the garrison of a fort in the Southwest would include two or three companies of the post commander's regiment, plus infantry and artillery companies. The forts commanded by Davidson often housed as many as twenty-five officers, of whom six to ten might be of the Tenth Cavalry. The record is quite clear that most of the officers, of all branches, who served under both commanders, preferred Davidson over Grierson. They considered Davidson to be a soldier's soldier. And the official records of General Davidson's thirty-six years of army service indicate that he was far more liked than disliked by subordinate officers. As for the enlisted men, they liked him, respected him, and felt confident when he led them into battle.

It is a well established fact that General Davidson fought the Indians on the western frontier ably and well, for a great many years. One might, therefore, be inclined to wonder about his attitude towards them. In that respect it is a fact that some military commanders of that era considered the Indians to be savages, and treated them with contempt. Insofar as this biographer can determine, Davidson always treated the Indians as warriors and respected them as such.

HOMER K. DAVIDSON

Acknowledgments

The preparation of this work is the result of almost five years of research in which the number of unpaid contributors is large. I wrote hundreds of letters inquiring about recorded activities of General Davidson. That was necessary because the pages of history mention him infrequently, and briefly. Adding to the difficulties was the fact that the general, himself, kept very few personal records, and he usually shunned publicity. Therefore, I corresponded with individuals, libraries, museums, historical societies, newspapers, and state and government archives. The majority of those contacted gave generously of their valuable time to locate interesting bits of information. To all of them I wish to express my sincere appreciation.

I have prowled through such museums as the Cavalry Museums at Fort Riley, Kansas and at Fort Bliss, Texas; the Post Museum at Fort Sill, Oklahoma; the Kit Carson Museum at Taos, New Mexico, and the Lincoln Memorial in Springfield, Illinois. In all cases the staff personnel were courteous and helpful. Then, too, the personnel of the Old Military Records Branch of National Archives in Washington, D.C., and of the Huntington Library in San Marino, California, were outstandingly helpful while I researched their collections.

I would like to pay an especial tribute to the publisher of the *Albany News* of Albany, Texas. That newspaper houses the only known substantial file of the old issues of one of its predecessors, the *Frontier Echo,* published at Jacksboro, Texas, which carried many references to the activities at Fort Richardson. The personnel of the *Albany News* expended many painstaking hours in poring through back issues of the *Echo* to provide me with valuable information about General Davidson.

Black Jack Davidson

West with the Howitzers

John W. Davidson was born in Fairfax County, Virginia, on August 14, 1825. He was the first of the four sons born to William B. and Elizabeth Davidson. The pages of history are filled with tales of men who were born with silver spoons in their mouths, but in this case there was a decided difference. The infant Davidson was, literally, born with a sword in his hand since he appeared at a time when the new Republic of the United States was being hammered together with the tools of warfare. The Revolutionary War was still vivid in the minds of the older generation, and the War of 1812 had ended just nine years earlier. Since the father had graduated from West Point in 1815, and was then serving as a second lieutenant in the Army, it is certain that military activities often became the chief topic of conversation in the Davidson household. It is only natural, therefore, that the new-born child inherited the military characteristics of his father, as well as those of his earlier ancestors on both sides of the family. His grandfather, William Lee Davidson,[1] served as a general officer during the Revolution and was killed in an engagement with the British Colonel Tarleton. The other grandfather, John Chapman Hunter, served in the Revolution as a private.

William B. Davidson served for twenty-five years,

---

[1] 49th Cong., 1 sess., *Senate Rept. 1306* (June 10, 1886), and *House Rept. 2943* (June 22, 1886).

following graduation from West Point, until he died on December 25, 1840, at Indian Key, Florida. At the time he was taking part in an operation in the Everglades, against Chief Chekika and his tribe. Lieutenant Colonel William S. Harney, the commander of the expedition, reported the death to the adjutant general of the Army in the following terms,

> Captain Davidson was unwell on leaving his post, but desirous of taking part in the expedition, concealed his indisposition from the Surgeon, and accompanied the command. On the third day after his departure, he was confined to his boat, and when landed at Indian Key, was beyond the reach of medical aid.

Knowing of his son's intense desire to enter West Point, Captain Davidson had written the following letter from Fort Lauderdale, on March 27, 1840, to the Secretary of War,

> Sir: I have the honor to request the appointment of Cadet for my son, John W. Davidson, who will present to you this letter, and for whom I respectfully solicit your very favorable consideration. He will, at the same time, hand you the testimonials he has named in reference to acquirement capacity and moral standing.

Many other letters from prominent individuals, including the adjutant general of the Army, also urged the appointment.

The long awaited appointment finally arrived and, on July 1, 1841, John W. Davidson entered West Point as a cadet, to begin a long, continuous and arduous career in the U.S. Army. Of that entrance it is interesting to note the following excerpt from his memoir, as written by an anonymous classmate for the 1882 class reunion,

> Rather small for his age, Davidson was well formed, neat in dress, handsome, and possessed of more maturity of manner and bearing than the average youth of his age. Albeit he was precise

in manners, Davidson was genial in temperament, fond of convivial amusements, and a favorite with his classmates, though, at times, somewhat testy, and ever ready to take offense. His academic career was in no wise different from that of the average cadet. He acquired with facility, and with little effort, a sufficient acquaintance with the prescribed curriculum to insure his graduation, and this satisfied his aspiration for academic honors.

The family military tradition was furthered when, on October 29, 1841, John's next older brother, Hunter Davidson, entered the U.S. Navy as acting midshipman.

John W. Davidson graduated from West Point on July 1, 1845, standing number twenty-seven in a class of forty. When asked which branch of the service he preferred he promptly requested assignment to the mounted services. That happened to be a natural choice for him since most Virginians grew up with a keen appreciation for good horseflesh, and took pride in having fine saddle horses. John's Virginia heritage, coupled with a natural aptitude for athletics and an enjoyment of certain kinds of physical exertion, certainly qualified him for the type of duty he preferred. In response to that request John was commissioned brevet second lieutenant, First Dragoons, and assigned to Fort Leavenworth, Kansas, where his regiment was then situated.

Davidson was highly elated when his assignment was announced, because he had fully expected to be ordered to the infantry. At that time there were but two mounted units in existence, and these were far below their authorized strength, due to the fact that sufficient funds had not been allotted for that purpose. As a consequence very few new assignments were being made to the Dragoons. Harking back to the close of the Revolutionary War, all mounted units were dropped from the army as unnecessary. That situation remained for about fifty years. Finally, in 1832, one regiment of mounted troops, the First Dragoons, was authorized in spite of strong opposition from certain factions in Congress. Although a second regiment was authorized some time later, the opposing Congressional faction was strong enough to block the additional funds needed for bringing the two regiments up to their required strength. This created a situation wherein the two regiments were tolerated on a "prove your value" basis. That limited and grudging approval of the two regiments was given only because of the necessity to provide protection to the supply trains that were constantly moving over the Santa Fe Trail. This protection had been too costly when provided by the infantry. When the Dragoons took over they soon demonstrated their ability to do the job better, and at lower cost. Even so their status was in constant jeopardy because of their opponents in Congress.

The First Dragoons were commanded by Colonel Stephen W. Kearny, who dedicated himself to the task of demonstrating the effectiveness of the Dragoons as guardians of the great plains of the west. He contended that the mobility of mounted soldiers provided the only effective means of combating the marauding Indians who ranged far and wide, and did so with great speed. The Dragoons of old had been lance and saber fighters, while the infantry used rifles. It became Kearny's policy, therefore, to combine the best of the two by providing the Dragoons with rifles, and train them to fight effectively either while mounted or on foot. That necessitated far more rigorous training, over a long period of time, for each recruit before he could be considered a competent "soldier on horseback." Under the watchful eye of Kearny the Dragoons ultimately developed into "hard riding, hard fighting" horsemen who were fiercely proud of their fast-growing reputation as "elite combat troops." That training also toughened them until they were capable of making long marches away from their garrisons, during which they endured the worst imaginable hardships. One of the things which had to be learned the "hard way" was that, in times of great need, mounted soldiers could subsist for days on horsemeat. They had to be prepared to kill some of the horses for their meat, a requirement that existed throughout the entire life of the United States horse cavalry.

The effectiveness of Kearny's method of training made such an impression on young Davidson that he never forgot it. In fact he adopted it as the basis for the future training of the troops under his command. As the years passed Davidson relied heavily on the Kearny method, adopting it entirely or modifying it to suit forthcoming missions, thus becoming noted for the capability of the troops he commanded. In later years, as the mounted services expanded, most of the cavalrymen were but vaguely familiar with the rudiments of fighting as infantrymen, but the soldiers under Davidson's command fought ably on foot as well as in the saddle.

A few months after arriving at Fort Leavenworth, Davidson, as a member of Company K, First Dragoons, received orders to proceed to Fort Crawford, Wisconsin. Their mission was to reinforce the existing small garrison, and to keep the very troublesome Sioux Indians in check. They departed from Fort Leavenworth early in February and arrived at Fort Crawford on March 31, 1846. The Indian menace subsided soon after the reinforcements arrived, and a relative degree of quiet prevailed for about two years. In fact the next outbreak did not occur until long after the First Dragoons returned to Fort Leavenworth. That particular uprising started in mid-1848 when the Indians launched an attack on New Ulm, Minnesota, and the townspeople had great difficulty in driving them off. While the Dragoons were at Fort Crawford they did not relax, instead they carried on a rigorous training program by making numerous reconnaissance patrols in the field. In this manner they gained a wealth of valuable information about the habits of the Indians, who were, at all times, potentially dangerous. That gave the Dragoons knowledge and experience that would serve them well much sooner than had been anticipated.

When the war with Mexico was declared, on May 12, 1846, Kearny received a new assignment. He was directed to command one of three armies that would be formed, each with a specific area of responsibility. They were: Army of Occupation commanded by Major General Zachary Taylor, Army of the Center commanded by Brigadier General John F. Wool, and the Army of the West commanded by Colonel Kearny. The assigned mission was for Kearny to organize his army at Fort Leavenworth, then march to Santa Fe and place the Mexican areas of New Mexico under the control of the United States. Upon completion of that operation he was to reform his army, in whatever strength was deemed necessary, and lead an expedition to California to bring the Mexican controlled portion of that area under the jurisdiction of the United States. When the latter operation was completed he should assume command as military governor.

Upon receipt of the directive to form his army, Kearny promptly ordered Company K to leave Fort Crawford forthwith, and to rejoin the regiment. Company K started out on their return to Fort Leavenworth on May 12, 1846, just about two days after Davidson received his promotion to a full-fledged second lieutenant. The marshaling of all available manpower was an urgent necessity for Kearny because, shortly before receiving orders to form his army he had, in response to a request to do so, sent all but about three hundred of his regiment to join the Second Dragoons. That was a necessary move so that the Second could be brought up to its full strength, and enable it to assist General Taylor's Army of Occupation then operating in the southwest corner of Texas.

Early in June 1846, large numbers of Missouri Volunteers began to flood into Fort Leavenworth to replace the First Dragoons who had left to join the Second. Practically all of the newcomers were raw recruits, with very little knowledge of the army. Therefore, it was necessary to mount an accelerated training program in order to prepare the unseasoned soldiers for the rigorous operations that would be encountered in the near future. The incoming troops consisted of a few mounted units, large numbers of infantry, and some artillery which swelled Kearny's total force to approximately sixteen hundred officers and men. One can be certain that the training program was such that it taxed the abilities and stamina of the regulars to the utmost.

While all of that feverish activity was in progress an interesting incident occurred, which has been repeated time and again when young men were taking part in a war. It demonstrates the high degree of concern that mothers have for their sons. The mother of Lieutenant Davidson, Mrs. Elizabeth C. Davidson, wrote to the Adjutant General of the Army expressing great concern for her son, from whom she had not heard for many months. Her letter, dated May 22, 1846, is on file with Adjutant General documents in National Archives.[2] The Adjutant General replied to Mrs. Davidson to the effect that her son was in good health and spirits.

Kearny's organization and training operations progressed so rapidly and well that he was ready to move in late June. He, therefore, set the date of departure from Fort Leavenworth as June 30, 1846, thus setting the stage for the conquest of New Mexico and California. It is certain that prospects of this adventure excited the interest and adventurous spirit of practically every man who was scheduled to participate. Although the two armies then operating in the Central and Southern sectors of Mexico were destined for everlasting fame for their achievements, the Army of the West faced one of the most difficult challenges ever undertaken by men. Before its task ended, Kearny's forces employed skill, ingenuity, devotion to duty, and just plain guts to a degree seldom equalled and never surpassed. Just before the force moved out of Fort Leavenworth a message arrived from the Secretary of War, advising Kearny that he would be promoted to brigadier general in the near future. Since he had served in the army for about thirty years, that news gave an enormous boost to Kearny's morale.

As the sun began to rise in the east, on June 30, 1846, the Army of the West left Fort Leavenworth, and

---

[2] Micro-film copy no. 567, roll 90-D.

headed for its first objective, Santa Fe. Since dragoon officers were trained to be highly versatile, Lieutenant Davidson drew the task of hauling four, two-wheeled, mountain howitzers, twelve-pounder size, and was given a small detachment for the job. It was his first command, but, since he happened to be the junior shavetail in the regiment, that distinction probably was somewhat dubious. Little did he know what the future held in store. The first phase of the march was uneventful, but exhausting, until July 20 when a near disaster struck. For the past several days some of the men suffered from a debilitating sickness that was not ordinarily serious. On the 20th, however, great anxiety prevailed because Kearny came down with it, and became seriously ill. This in addition to the one hundred or so who were already on the doctors' lists. Nevertheless the march continued, at Kearny's insistence, and the sick gradually improved. By July 29 most of the ill were back on their feet, and the crossing of the Arkansas River was made. Thus the expedition stepped on Mexican soil for the first time, somewhere in the vicinity of Bent's Fort where supplies awaited their arrival. Kearny realized that a far more rigorous march lay ahead, so he decided to camp for a few days to allow men and animals to regain their strength and vigor. In taking stock of their performance to date Kearny calculated that about six hundred miles had been covered, for an average of more than twenty miles per day. That constituted a near record for the movement of such a large force – more than sixteen hundred men – over unfamiliar territory.

Following a most welcome rest the march was resumed on August 2 and, fulfilling their expectations, the going became increasingly difficult. They slowly inched along and, while crossing the "Great American Desert," the animals suffered to the point of exhaustion. Some of them had to be abandoned. After the "Desert" was crossed the force began to ascend the Raton, a most arduous climb over the rugged chain of mountains which separates the Arkansas and Canadian rivers. At an altitude of seventy-five hundred feet the bone-weary men began the descent. Although they moved downward at a faster pace, the going was actually more difficult than the climb. Many sharp spurs, formed by the channel of the mountain stream, were encountered on this, the only possible trail suitable for the passage of the heavy wagons and artillery. Once again the food supplies ran low, forcing all personnel to subsist on half rations. More seriously, however, there was insufficient forage for the horses and mules, causing many of them to play out and be abandoned. To the everlasting credit of the men who formed that expedition was the fact that they managed to retain a good sense of humor, making jokes about their difficulties. It is doubtful that the force could have negotiated that particular stretch of the march if they had lacked their grim sense of humor.[3] The entire force received a substantial boost in morale when, on August 16, official orders caught up with them and, among other things, contained Kearny's commission as brigadier general.

Two days later, with brand new stars shining on his shoulders, Kearny rode into Santa Fe at the head of a large body of soldiers who fully expected to meet stiff resistance. Instead, the force received a rousing welcome. Although the Volunteers seemed to be greatly

---

[3] N. C. Brooks, *History of the Mexican War,* chapter 14.

relieved at the lack of opposition, it was evident that the Dragoons were disappointed. Those regulars, who were trained to fight, had not seen action for a long time and were spoiling for a good scrap. Nevertheless, harmony prevailed and the American flag replaced the Mexican colors atop the Governor's Palace without one word of dissension.[4] The raising of that flag heralded the culmination of an epic performance. The Army of the West had marched from Fort Leavenworth to Santa Fe in just fifty days, over eight hundred and eighty miles of arid desert, through extremely rugged mountains, and other terrain that was, at times, nearly impassable due to floods or rock slides. The route they followed from Bent's Fort to Santa Fe is, incidentally, almost identical to the one used many years later by the Santa Fe Railroad.

On the Thursday, August 27, following the march into the city a celebration ball was held in the Governor's Palace. It was attended by all the officers of the expedition, and most of the ladies and gentlemen of the community. The festivities started with a sumptuous meal of many courses, and copious quantities of wine. As the evening progressed both men and women lit up fierce-looking black cigars, or cigarillos. The smoke curled into the room in great clouds making the air so dense that breathing became difficult, especially for those men who were accustomed to living in the open air. It eventually became so bad that Kearny, himself, was overcome with sickness which forced him to leave the party and take to his bed. Nevertheless, it was a gala event that did a great deal to establish a good rapport

---

[4] It is not the purpose of this work to comment upon or analyze the successful negotiations which preceded the actual conquest of Santa Fe.

between the "invaders" and the residents of the city. While the ball in the Governor's Palace was going on the soldiers were also entertained. At their dinner they were introduced to totally unfamiliar foods. For example, huge quantities of chili was served, so peppery hot that it burned the throats of the soldiers, and forced them to cool the blazing heat with generous quantities of wine and rum. As a consequence everybody had fun that night, and very little useful work was performed the next morning.

Since there was a lull in the required activities, the trail-weary troops were allowed to take it easy for the first few days in Santa Fe. That because Kearny firmly believed it to be vitally important for his soldiers to rest, and regain their strength before starting the next phase of the mission. When he did start preparing for the onward march he demanded the utmost effort from every man. All of the intelligence then available indicated that the route ahead consisted of mountains and deserts worse than those recently traversed. He was advised that horses probably would not have enough stamina for the rugged route ahead, and that mules should be substituted since they were much hardier than horses. Kearny, therefore, weeded out most of the horses and at the same time made a careful study of his personnel requirements. He came to the conclusion that better progress could be made if he divided the total force into two units. One of the units, to go with Kearny, was composed of the Dragoons under Major Sumner, a small group of Topographical Engineers under Lieutenant Emory, and the howitzer detachment under Lieutenant Davidson, to a total of about three hundred. The second unit, to be led by Lieutenant Colonel Philip St. George

Cooke, would follow later and build a road as it moved along. Before leaving Santa Fe, Cooke would arrange for a garrison force to remain in the city.

All preparations were completed in record time, and the advance expedition marched out of Santa Fe on September 25, 1846, with General Kearny at its head. They followed the Rio Grande to Albuquerque, then crossed to the west bank and continued moving south. As expected, it was rough going every step of the way, and frequent stops were necessary in order to rest the hard-working animals. On October 6, Kearny intercepted Kit Carson, then a temporary lieutenant, who was en route to Washington with urgent dispatches from Commodore Stockton and Lieutenant Colonel Fremont in California. The messages contained information to the effect that the Mexicans had surrendered to a combined force of sailors from Stockton's squadron and soldiers from Fremont's expedition. Carson had been picked to make the dangerous dash to Washington with the good news because of his experience as a guide, and an intimate knowledge of the far western country. Later events proved the news to be premature and that the dispatches had been sent impulsively, because the Mexicans soon rebelled against the handful of occupying Americans and regained control. Kearny, however, was unaware of the actual situation in California, but did recognize the urgent nature of the messages being carried by Carson. After studying the situation, and conferring with Carson and the Dragoon officers, Kearny decided that his meager knowledge of the route to California should be fortified by a man with Carson's expertise. He, therefore, directed Carson to join his expedition, and assigned another man to follow through with the delivery of the dispatches. Carson objected vehemently, but Kearny's will prevailed and the Army of the West gained the services of a guide who knew the route ahead as well as any living white man.

Kearny, Carson and all the Dragoon officers sat down to thoroughly discuss the forthcoming march to California, with especial consideration given to the latest news from there. At best, the route ahead was a formidable one, and Carson was fully aware of the difficulties involved in moving a large force over it because forage for the animals would be scarce. In order to reduce those problems to a minimum everyone agreed that it would be best to pare everything down to bare essentials. That meant a sharp reduction in the size of the force, as well as the quantity of supplies, equipment and vehicles. Kearny then decided that the ongoing force would be composed of one hundred Dragoons, the Topographical Engineers, and the howitzer detachment. Considerable opposition to the inclusion of the howitzers was voiced, but Kearny insisted they would be needed later. Certainly he must have regretted that decision long before reaching California. The Dragoons were divided into two companies of just under fifty men each, and the howitzer detachment. One civilian, a Mr. Robideaux, joined the force as interpreter. The grand total came to one hundred and twenty-five. The remaining Dragoons, about two hundred, with Major Sumner in charge were directed to return to Santa Fe. Later events proved that the return of the Dragoons to Santa Fe was a mistake, because Kearny would, eventually, need every able-bodied soldier he could muster. However, based upon the information then available, the decision was sound, especially since it was understood that a full regiment was en route to California by boat.

As the officer-in-charge of the mountain howitzers, Lieutenant Davidson embarked upon a close association with the famous Kit Carson – one that continued intermittently for about ten years. During that time the two often fought side by side in numerous skirmishes with Indians. Many years later Carson wrote, in his memoirs, that he well knew Davidson and considered him to be one of the most fearless and capable officers he knew.

Before breaking camp, on October 6, 1846, Carson had another talk with Kearny to outline, as graphically as possible, the difficulties that would be encountered in the mountains and on the desert, and the increasingly rough country they would cover. He followed this with a strong recommendation to abandon the cumbersome wagons, and carry all supplies on pack mules. He said that, in his opinion, they could not hope to reach California in less than four months in any other manner. Kearny, however, was reluctant to deprive his men and animals of the few small conveniences that wagon-borne supplies could provide, and decided to retain the vehicles. The expedition started the onward march to California, still heading in a southerly direction. Within two days the going became so rough that some of the wagons broke down and most of the teams were blown. They made camp again, on October 9, and remained for four days while mules were procured, and loaded with the most essential supplies and equipment. Everything else was abandoned, and the march resumed. At that time the only vehicles that remained were two, two-wheeled howitzers which Kearny had insisted upon retaining as potentially necessary weapons.

On October 14 the expedition left the Rio Grande at

a point about ten miles north of the small town of Cuchillo, New Mexico, and started moving in a westerly direction. They plodded on over a table-land, and approached the Sierra de los Mimbres through a beautiful area that was well laced with small streams, and covered with a lush growth of grass and trees. For the next few days the animals had good grazing, and the men found that the region provided good hunting and fishing. Needless to say, every man and animal took full advantage of the excellent nourishment so generously provided by nature. The force arrived at the rich Santa Rita copper mines on October 18. They learned that the mines had been abandoned sometime previously, because all the miners' supply routes had been cut by the Apache Indians. Much to the surprise of all hands the party was greeted by Chief Red Sleeve, who offered a pact of friendship and freedom from attack. Although both Kearny and Carson were skeptical of the chief's offers, peaceful conditions did prevail, and the force moved onward without molestation by the small bands of Apaches who roamed throughout the area. The Indians even visited the camp each night to trade with the soldiers. One night a fat, middle-aged squaw tried to trade one of the troopers out of the red flannel shirt he was wearing, but the soldier would not part with it. She then mounted her pony and galloped around the camp at full speed, screaming at the top of her voice and shedding her clothes until stark naked. She continued riding in the all-together until a deal was finally made for a red shirt. That was probably the first strip-tease performance in the far west.

The onward movement became more difficult by the hour as the hardy Dragoons worked their way up and across the Continental Divide. Altitudes of seven thousand feet and more were reached while the temperatures dropped sharply. The nights were bitterly cold, forcing the men and their mounts to huddle together around roaring campfires in order to keep warm. They must have rued the day when so many of their warm blankets and various items of heavy clothing had been sent back to Santa Fe with Major Sumner. During the day the sun blazed down on them in full force, thus subjecting the soldiers and their mounts to daily changes in temperature, ranging from very hot to bitter cold. The route now being followed took them through an almost impenetrable labyrinth of mountain spurs, narrow tortuous paths paved with sharp fragments of flint-like rock, and deep ravines. The whole was often thickly overgrown with mesquite, cactus, and other shrubs that tore at clothing and lacerated their skin. Gila monsters and other poisonous creatures constantly menaced them with their venom. Happy, indeed, were those struggling soldiers when they broke out of the mountains on November 9, and started descending to the valley of the Gila River. At that point it was a stream about fifty feet wide and two feet deep, with clear and cold water running very fast over a pebbled bed. It was bordered on both sides with trees and high-rising mountains.

The scenery, as described in the official log, was gorgeous as the expedition marched along the river. But the going got more difficult as they progressed, with the trail frequently pinching down to a narrow canyon, causing them to travel along the boulder-strewn river bed. Passage over this trail was, at times, almost impossible, and young Davidson with his heavy two-wheeled vehicles faced problems that taxed his inge-

nuity to the utmost. There were many occasions when
he was forced to dismantle the howitzers, load them on
pack mules, then re-assemble them when it became possible to use wheels again. This small detachment seldom
made camp each night until very late, and sometimes
not until the next day. A couple of times Kearny lay
over in camp for a day to allow the late-arriving howitzer detachment an opportunity to recuperate from its
strenuous efforts of the preceding night. Carson and the
senior officers tried to convince Kearny that the howitzers should be abandoned, to permit an increase in their
speed. He, however, insisted that those weapons would
ultimately be vital to their survival, and decided to keep
them if humanly possible. It was thus that Lieutenant
Davidson, and his small detachment, performed an operation seldom equalled and never surpassed for sheer
determination, brute strength, and raw courage in the
face of indescribable hardship, in accomplishing a
seemingly impossible task. Those men dragged, carried,
pushed and lifted those mountain howitzers across
mountains, through ravines, and over desert wastes to
chalk up a record. Their two howitzers went down in
history as the first wheeled vehicles to cross the area of
Arizona. Of that performance Doctor Griffin, the accompanying army Surgeon, wrote in his diary,

> These are the only wheeled vehicles we have along, and they are
> about as much trouble as all the packs put together. . . the
> howitzers have not come up yet, and it is 8 p.m. . . Poor
> Davidson is having a hell of a time of it.

Similar remarks appear in the official log which was
maintained by Lieutenant Emory, the head of the Topographical Engineers. By any standard of measurement, it must have been an epic performance.

Of course Davidson was not the only one with difficult problems to contend with. As they moved ahead, mules were lost because of complete exhaustion and, eventually, Kearny lost his horse which was the only one remaining with the expedition. He too had to ride a mule, and that balky animal often refused to move – Kearny would be forced to dismount and push the contrary beast while a trooper pulled. The expedition trudged onward for a distance of some three hundred miles, through long stretches of grassless desert, long climbs up the sides of mountains, and through parched valleys and tablelands that contained nothing but a few scattered, stunted growths as the only vegetation. Lieutenant Emory wrote of this many times in his official log, which was entitled "Notes of a military reconnoissance from Fort Leavenworth to San Diego." One such entry summed up the entire situation that faced them daily, as follows,

> We found ourselves some thousand feet above the River, traveled sixteen miles then down again. It was over eight hours of hard labor. The whole day was a succession of steep ascents and descents, paved with sharp, angular fragments of basalt and trap.

Even the mules, normally not too particular about their diet, would not touch the bitter and offensive shrubs that grew along the way. Occasionally a bit of bottom land afforded pitifully small bits of forage for the mules. Eventually these hardy animals began to play out, and some were lost completely.

At long last the expedition arrived at the juncture of the Gila with the Colorado River, on November 22, 1846. The mules were half dead, and the commissary was empty. The long march had also taken its toll of the men. They were exhausted, their clothing was in tatters, their skin badly lacerated from the cactus tearing at them, and shoes were at the point of falling from their feet. The rapidly-flowing, clear waters of the Colorado were a welcome sight indeed. Kearny planned to stop here for several days to allow both men and animals to recuperate. However, he received information that about one hundred Mexicans, with some five hundred horses, were camped within a few miles. They were en route to Mexico to deliver the horses to the Mexican Army. Since his expedition badly needed healthy mounts Kearny organized a surprise attack, and overcame the Mexicans, capturing the horses, blankets, supplies, and other useful equipment. Unfortunately, however, the horses proved to be of little value, since they were untrained and mostly wild.

On the person of one of the Mexican officers a number of dispatches and letters were found and opened. From these Kearny learned that a counter-revolution had occurred in California shortly after Carson left there with the urgent dispatches for Washington. The Americans had been expelled from Santa Barbara, Los Angeles, and several other places. Kearny decided to break camp as soon as possible and proceed posthaste to California. Early on the morning of November 25, 1846, at a point about ten miles south of the campsite, the expedition forded the Colorado River and set foot on California soil for the first time. The grazing was very good on the west bank of the river, and every possible advantage was taken of the bonanza. Animals were allowed to stuff themselves on the succulent grass, and each man tied huge bundles of it to his saddle before starting into the desert.

When the expedition moved on, they headed into a

dreary waste of white, yellow and brown sand that stretched ahead for nearly ninety miles, and as far to each side as the eye could see. There was no known water for at least thirty miles. While moving across the desert the scorching hot sun blinded their eyes, and the reflected heat from the sand was so intense that it sunburned the under sides of their chins. Seldom has man endured such misery as that hardy group suffered while crossing that desert. They shuffled and plodded along for about twenty-four miles, then halted at the "Alamo," a large dry gully. Here they dug two holes about fifteen feet deep, and found enough brackish water to satisfy immediate needs. It was far from palatable, but a relief nevertheless.

The march was resumed the next morning, and the men struggled along swearing, sweating, gritting their teeth, and dreaming of the wonderfully cool waters of the Colorado River that was far behind. The pack mules often sank into the sand and, being exhausted, could not get free. The men, who were ravenously hungry, slaughtered those unfortunate animals and ate their meat, which was unsalted, tough, stringy and wholly unpalatable. Difficult as it was, they managed to down enough of the meat to sustain their strength and keep them going. Thirty-two of the most grueling miles imaginable were covered that day. Of this experience Captain Johnson, First Dragoons, wrote in his diary: "Poor fellows, they are well nigh naked, some barefoot, a sorry looking lot."

Kearny pushed ahead as rapidly as humanly possible for the next twenty-two miles to the next watering place, Cariso [Carrizo] Creek. Refreshed by these waters the force moved on, following a road that was slightly less

difficult than the desert sands. However, it took them
through dense thickets of century plant containing sharp
spears that tore at the clothing and flesh of the bone-
weary men. They soon experienced another shortage of
food which compelled the slaughter of more mules for
meat. In the Imperial Valley the expedition turned
northward, passing the Alkali Sink, now known as the
Salton Sea. After that their progress gradually improved as they neared the mountains.

The desert was finally left behind on November 28,
as they passed through a mountain gap in a dense fog.
At that time the misery of the nearly-exhausted Dragoons changed radically. The increasing altitude, as
they trudged up the mountains, brought on cold, ice-
laden winds that whipped through their torn and scant
clothing, cutting into their bones like needle-sharp
icicles. The miracle of it is that these trail-hardened
Dragoons survived the sudden change in climate, from
one extreme to the other, without developing a single
case of illness that could be considered serious.

Eight days after fording the Colorado River the expedition arrived at the Rancho of Jose Warner, near
Palomar Mountain, on December 2, 1846. They were,
indeed, a fierce looking lot, bedraggled, hungry, and
suffering from badly bruised and lacerated skin. In fact
they looked so desperate that the ranch vaqueros herded
all the cattle into the hills for their protection. Perhaps
that was a wise move, because it was reported that seven
of the famished Dragoons ate a whole sheep at one
sitting.

2

California Duty

Upon the arrival of the expedition at Jose Warner's Rancho, Kearny lost no time in sending an urgent dispatch to Commodore Stockton, then in San Diego. In that message he described the near-desperate condition of his troops, that they were suffering from overexposure, malnutrition, severe colds, and their clothing was in tatters. He also outlined his desperate need for ammunition, boots, clothing, provisions and arms. For some unaccountable reason Stockton replied that he could not comply with the request for assistance. Kearny was thus forced to make-do with whatever he could obtain from the residents of the area, and from the land, which was barely enough to sustain life. It is fortunate, indeed, that the rigors of the past months had provided the men of the expedition with an abundance of resourcefulness. They searched the countryside and fared reasonably well, insofar as immediate needs were concerned, but nothing for a reserve supply.

While Kearny was endeavoring to decide upon his next move, information reached him that a Mexican detachment was encamped nearby with a consignment of about one hundred horses for delivery to the Mexican commander in Sonora, General Flores. The leader of the detachment was an aristocrat named Don Antonio Coronel, who was one of Flores' insurgents. Kearny detailed a small group, about one squad of Dragoons, commanded by Lieutenant Davidson with Kit Carson as guide, to go out and round up the animals and bring them into camp. The raiding party started at daybreak, and ranged over a great deal of the surrounding countryside before locating their quarry. The Mexicans were in a camp where their leader had found shelter in an Indian hut. It was the cold, rainy night of December 3, 1846, and Coronel had just removed his clothes for drying when Davidson charged the camp. Coronel, unceremoniously, took to his heels, wearing nothing but a nightshirt. A short, sharp skirmish ensued, but the Mexicans lacked any desire for a fight and the action ended almost before it started. The intrepid Dragoons proceeded to round up the entire lot of horses and mules, then headed back to their own camp. They arrived about noon on the 4th, and presented the animals to Kearny. Unfortunately, only some thirty of the total number of animals could be considered serviceable as mounts, but that many were a welcome addition to a force which lacked enough mounts for all of its personnel.

As soon as possible after Davidson returned, Kearny broke camp and set out for San Diego in a hard and bitterly cold rain. Those poorly clad and somewhat emaciated soldiers were just about as miserable as human beings could be. Nevertheless, they slogged ahead through the mud and slush until a point was reached near the Rancheria San Pasqual, about seven miles southeast of Escondido, where they made camp. Intelligence soon arrived indicating that a large number of Mexican soldiers, commanded by Captain Andres Pico, was camped across their trail, just a short distance ahead. Kearny studied the situation from all angles, concluding that his best course would be to capitalize upon the element of surprise, and launch an immediate attack. Since the Dragoons had been spoiling for a fight, their exhaustion was completely forgotten and they charged enthusiastically. Their initial attack produced the desired results, as the Mexicans retreated in a great rush. Sensing a complete victory the overly-eager troopers pursued the fleeing Mexicans too far. When one thinks of that battle it is relatively easy to visualize the utter incongruity of that poorly armed force, mounted for the most part on mules, charging into a much larger organization of well-mounted, well-armed soldiers who were excellent horsemen.

The Dragoons hotly pursued the fleeing Mexicans for a few miles, without realizing that reinforcements had reached the enemy. Captain Pico then counterattacked, and the resulting melee was short, and nearly disastrous for Kearny's force. During the fracas Davidson managed to maneuver the two howitzers into position for firing, but one of the teams bolted. The alert Mexicans chased, and lassoed the run-aways, captured the howitzer, and hauled it off about three hundred yards. At that point they attempted to unlimber the gun for use against the Americans, but without success because none of them understood the firing mechanism. While the Mexicans were hauling the gun away Davidson followed in hot pursuit, in an attempt to recapture the howitzer, and ran headlong into the thick of the fight. During all this action Davidson lost all of his men, one howitzer, and very nearly lost his own life in the process. He was lanced through his clothing several times, with one lance barely missing a vital spot when it passed through his shirt to lodge in the cantle of his saddle.

When the skirmish finally ended it was found to be a disaster of major proportions for Kearny's forces. Nineteen of the Dragoons were killed, fifteen wounded, plus Kearny who was badly injured by two lance thrusts. Three of his officers and four of the noncoms were among those killed. When camp was made that night the dead were buried, and Doctor Griffin, the force surgeon, had his skill taxed to the utmost in patching up the wounded and trying to keep them alive. Kearny had no means of counting the losses sustained by Captain Pico's forces, since their expert horsemanship enabled them to carry off the casualties before any count could be made. Nevertheless, the indications were that he had suffered a great many losses in both dead and wounded. However, that did not lessen the desperate nature of the Americans' situation, since further attacks by the Mexicans seemed a certainty. In such an event the badly decimated Dragoons probably could not hope to survive without reinforcements. Kearny, therefore, sent three men to San Diego, thirty miles away, with an urgent plea for help. Although historians have labeled that attack by the Americans as ill-advised, they are rendering judgements based upon hindsight. Kearny, as the field commander on that cold, wet night of December 6, 1846, believed it to be the only course of action that could properly be taken. That skirmish is recorded in the official records as the "Battle of San Pasqual."

All through the night of the 6th, Doctor Griffin labored in an effort to administer to the needs of the injured who were, incidentally, itching for another chance at the Mexicans. Although they were exhausted from their strenuous efforts, and had not slept for more than thirty hours, they were too keyed up to do any sleeping that night. When dawn broke, this little force, now about one third its original size, ragged, weak, and with most of their mounts dead or lame, prepared to move on to San Diego. Once again the lack of provisions forced them to resort to the highly disagreeable flesh of slaughtered mules. As soon as they were all on the trail to San Diego the Mexican troops swooped down on them in great force. The odds seemed insurmountable yet those rough and ready Dragoons fought their way through enemy lines to the Rancheria Bernardo, and took up a position on a hill. They were then about twenty miles from San Diego, in a situation that appeared to be more desperate than ever. At this time Kearny dispatched Kit Carson and Lieutenant Beale to San Diego with another urgent plea for reinforcements. It is fortunate that he did so, because the first three messengers did not get through the Mexican lines. For the next four days Kearny and his small band of Dragoons fought off the repeated attacks that were vigorously launched by Pico's troops. All during that siege the Dragoons had nothing but mule meat to eat, so they named their little hilltop stronghold "Mule Hill." It is so commemorated by an historical marker at the foot of the hill.

On the morning of the fifth day Navy Lieutenant Gray, with a force of one hundred and fifty Navy and Marine Corps personnel joined the beleaguered Dragoons. Captain Pico soon learned of this and withdrew his forces; some historians maintain that he fled precipitately. The reinforcements from San Diego brought clothing, arms, ammunition and provisions. For the first time in many long weeks the Dragoons dressed warmly, had their fill of good food, and felt that they had finally landed in the lap of luxury. On the forenoon of December 11, Kearny resumed his march and arrived in San Diego the following day. This terminated a march of two and one-half months' duration, which covered one thousand and ninety miles of country that was, at times, almost impassable. Complete rest, recuperation, and the doctoring of wounds was the most important order of business. For these precious few days the bone-weary Dragoons took full advantage of the comfortable lodgings and sumptuous meals that were provided by the San Diego garrison.

After the period of rest Kearny began preparations to complete his mission, which was to capture the territorial capital of Los Angeles, and place it under U.S. jurisdiction. Around the hard core of able-bodied and tough Dragoons he assembled a small army of new recruits, plus sailors, marines, and artillery. The total strength of this newly constituted Army of the West rapidly swelled to about five hundred. The Dragoons pitched in with a will in an effort to instill some of their pride and know-how in the newcomers. Of course those Dragoons had every reason to be proud of their recent accomplishments, in out-fighting and out-maneuvering a vastly superior force of well-equipped Mexican soldiers. Little did they realize that historians would credit them with one of the finest examples of sheer courage and fighting ability. At the moment, however, their enthusiasm was infectious, and the recruits soon developed into acceptable replacements for the ones who had fallen.

Kearny set out at the head of his formidable army on December 29, 1846, and headed for Los Angeles. Progress was unusually slow, due to the cumbersome supply wagons, and the San Gabriel River was not reached until January 8, 1847. Their crossing of that river was opposed by a force of more than seven hundred Mexican soldiers, commanded by General Flores. A spirited skirmish ensued before the Americans could successfully cross the river. In the process Kearny's army suffered no serious casualties and, at the end of about two hours of hard fighting, were the undisputed masters of the field. The tired but elated soldiers made camp for the night at the scene of the battle. History records it as one of the major engagements in the conquest of California, and designates it, "The Passage of the San Gabriel."

The following morning the Army of the West started across the wide plain between the San Gabriel and Los Angeles rivers, while the enemy continually harrassed them with hit and run attacks on their flank. At the crest of a ravine the Mexicans massed for a last ditch stand at a distance of about four miles from the town of Los Angeles. They made a brisk charge at full gallop, and were met by a strong counter-attack. The resulting melee was vicious but brief, and the numerically superior forces of General Flores were put to rout. From there Flores fled to Sonora, Mexico. In the battle two Americans were killed; several were wounded, but not seriously. Once again the highly superior horsemanship of the Mexicans enabled them to remove their casualties before a head count could be made. However, there was every reason to believe that Flores had suffered major losses, estimated to be close to eighty-five. That engagement occurred on January 9, 1847, and was officially designated as the "Battle of the Plains of the Mesa." It is commemorated by an historical marker in front of the Union Stockyards headquarters building, in the city of Vernon, California.

After the smoke of battle cleared away, Kearny ordered his army to pitch camp for the night, to spruce up their equipment and persons. The next morning the Army of the West was assembled with fifty proud and smart-looking Dragoons in the van as the triumphant march into Los Angeles began. The Dragoons had, incidentally, been on foot ever since they left San Diego because of a dire shortage of suitable mounts. It was a smart-looking army, indeed, that marched into the territorial capital, without encountering the slightest opposition from the townspeople. It was in this glorious manner that the final chapter of one of the greatest epics in the history of the United States ended – General Stephen Watts Kearny's expedition to California. Less than half of the one hundred and twenty-five hand-picked men who had set out from Socorro, New Mexico, more than three months earlier, were present when the American flag was hoisted over the city of Los Angeles on January 10. The *History of the Mexican War* by N. C. Brooks, in the chapter entitled "Army of the West," records their performance in this manner: "The story of those months has yet, in military annals, to find a parallel."

In addition to their many feats of endurance and heroism, these two firsts are credited to the Kearny Expedition:[1]

1. They were the first to bring wheeled vehicles across the State of Arizona.
2. Doctor John Strother Griffin, Assistant Surgeon U.S. Army, was the first fully accredited doctor to set foot in California.

---

[1] John K. Herr, *The Story of the U.S. Cavalry.*

On March 17, 1847, Lieutenant Colonel Philip St. George Cooke, who was directed to follow Kearny, marched into Los Angeles with his large force, composed mostly of Mormon volunteers. They had, during the march, laid out a roadway for future use. Upon arrival Cooke was placed in command of the Southern Military District, in order to lighten Kearny's rapidly increasing load of responsibilities. It is well that this assignment had been made, because a quarrel developed between Kearny on the one hand, and Stockton and Fremont on the other, over who would be the superior military authority in California. Since Fremont was the more antagonistic of the two, his actions culminated in his trial by court-martial, somewhat later, on the charge of insubordination. In the meantime Kearny's will prevailed and, backed by his original orders from Washington, he functioned as the military commander.

A short time prior to the arrival of Cooke in Los Angeles, work had been started on a fort, located on what was later designated Fort Hill. It was intended to house one hundred men, but construction had barely started before the entire project was abandoned. However, in April rumors reached Kearny that Mexican General Bustamente, with a large army, was marching on Los Angeles to drive the Americans out. Precautions were immediately taken to meet the threat, and troops were dispersed in strategic locations around the city. In addition, the military commander decided to construct a fort that would be much larger than the one originally planned, and locate it on the site selected a few months earlier. This would provide adequate protection for the city.

Lieutenant J. W. Davidson, First Dragoons, was assigned to the task of planning and constructing the new fort, and a battalion of Mormon volunteers detailed to do the work. Since the plans that had been drawn up for the original layout were not available, a short period of time was necessary for preparing new ones. The actual construction began on April 23, 1847, on Fort Hill, just three months after work on the first fort had stopped. The records are not clear about the amount of construction that had been accomplished in the first effort, but the time element suggests that little more than a small amount of land clearing could have been done. A few days after construction started, Colonel J. D. Stevenson, with a regiment of New York volunteers, arrived in California. It is possible that news of this reinforcement reached General Bustamente and caused him to change his plans. What happened may never be known, but it is a fact that he suddenly abandoned his plan to recapture Los Angeles, and began moving back toward Mexico. Nevertheless, the work of building the new fort continued without interruption.

Lieutenant Colonel Cooke resigned his position on May 13, 1847, and Colonel Stevenson succeeded him as commander of the Southern Military District. One of the new commander's first acts was to direct the procurement for the fort, of a flagpole that would reach a suitable height. That posed a difficult problem because there were no trees nearby that would satisfy his requirements for a pole at least one hundred and fifty feet high. A detail was sent to the San Bernardino Mountains where trees were located that would be suitable, provided two were spliced together. They were brought to Los Angeles, where the carpenters did the splicing job, and produced a one-hundred-and-fifty-foot pole.

That flagstaff was raised on the grounds of the fort, at a location that approximates the present-day southeast corner of North Broadway and Fort Moore Place.

By the first day of July the work on the fort had progressed far enough for Colonel Stevenson to declare the Fourth of July as the date for dedication. His official order for the dedication, that celebrated the birthday of the American Independence, is paraphrased as follows,

> At sunrise a Federal salute will be fired from the field work on the hill which commands this town, and for the first time from this point the American standard will be displayed. At 10 o'clock every soldier at this post will be under arms. The detachment of the 7th Regiment, New York Volunteers and 1st Regiment, U.S. Dragoons, dismounted, will be marched to the field work on the hill, when together with the Mormon Battalion, the whole will be formed at 11 o'clock a.m. into a hollow square when the Declaration of Independence will be read. At the close of this ceremony the field work will be dedicated and appropriately named; and at 12 o'clock a national salute will be fired. The field work at this post having been planned, and the work conducted entirely by Lieutenant Davidson of the First Dragoons, he is requested to hoist upon it for the first time, on the morning of the 4th, the American Standard. The Fort shall bear the name of Moore, in honor of Captain B. D. Moore, Company A, First Dragoons, who lost his life in the Battle of San Pasqual.

The Declaration of Independence was read in English, then in Spanish. The native Californians, seated on their horses in the rear of the soldiers, listened and considered it to be a *pronunciamento* which, in effect, it was. The fort extended for nearly four hundred feet, contained a breastwork for cannons, and would accommodate a force of more than two hundred. It was described as being in a strong position, and could easily have defended against an attack by one thousand. Its rear was protected by a deep ravine running diagonally from the cemetery to Spring Street, just south of Temple. The fort remained in full operation until 1849 when it was abandoned.[2] Fort Hill was, incidentally, leveled in 1949 for real-estate developments. Much of the area once known as Fort Moore is now (1973) occupied by the Los Angeles Board of Education buildings.

Prior to the completion of Fort Moore, Kearny received orders from Washington to return to Fort Leavenworth for a new assignment. He left Los Angeles on May 31, 1847, and his replacement, Colonel R. B. Mason, moved the headquarters to Monterey, California. He took a large portion of the Dragoons with him, but detachments remained in the Los Angeles area. Among those remaining was Lieutenant Davidson, who became the Chief Quartermaster Officer for the Southern Army District shortly after he completed his work on Fort Moore. Although the duties in the new assignments were active and highly responsible, they were a welcome relief from the physically exhausting field activities he had experienced since leaving Fort Leavenworth. Relative quiet prevailed throughout California for the remainder of 1847, which gave the Dragoons an excellent opportunity to build their units to full authorized strength, and turn them into effective fighting organizations.

The peaceful atmosphere in California began to change for the worse when, on January 28, 1848, gold was discovered at Sutter's Mill near Sacramento. Almost immediately gold seekers started pouring into the area in ever increasing numbers. As was to be expected, the gold seekers were followed by large numbers of

---

[2] J. M. Guinn, *Historical and Biographical Record of Los Angeles.*

parasites, prostitutes, murderers, bandits, gamblers and others who were eager to relieve the miners of the fruits of their labors. That triggered a wave of lawlessness that taxed the resources of both the military and civilian peace-keeping activities to the utmost. It was hoped that the signing of the Treaty of Guadalupe Hidalgo on February 2, 1848, which ended the conflict with Mexico, would enable the newly-constituted California government to stabilize the situation. It was wishful thinking, however, for the number of robberies, murders, and other lawless acts increased to the point where all of the peace-keeping forces were over-extended. Local police and the military units in that vicinity found themselves unable to respond to all the desperate calls for help that flooded in. Lynch law prevailed in several localities. As if that wasn't bad enough, Indian hostilities began to spread rapidly throughout the entire northern part of the territory. Colonel Mason responded to the situation by ordering Company C, First Dragoons, to move from Los Angeles to Fort Sonoma. With Captain Smith in command and Lieutenant Davidson the next ranking officer, that Company, now at full strength, well equipped and well trained, arrived in Sonoma in mid-May 1849.

The situation then existing in California is best described by the following excerpts from a report to the Adjutant General, U.S. Army, from Colonel R. B. Mason, First Dragoons, dated December 27, 1848,

> The regiment (First Dragoons), you are aware, has been strung from Sonoma in the north, to San Jose in Lower California, during their whole time of service in this quarter. The companies stationed at La Paz (Steele's and Matsell's) held that town for many weeks against four times their numbers, and the very moment they were reinforced by Nagle's company, with additional

recruits, they took the field, under the command of Lt. Col. Burton, routed the enemy, completely dispersed him, and restored peace to the Peninsula. . .

2. Now that the War with Mexico is over I feel it due to the officers of the army, who have served and still serve under my command, to draw your attention to the services they have rendered to the Government. They have obeyed the orders of their Government, and by careful and strict attention to their appropriate duties have maintained quiet and order among the most confused element of society. Heavy and responsible duties devolved upon Captain Folsom as assistant Quartermaster and Collector of Customs at San Francisco, and they have been well performed. Captain Smith and Lieut. Davidson of the Dragoons, Lieuts. Ord and Loeser of the Artillery have been faithful and constant on duty with their respective companies. Lieut. Davidson has also been on duty as chief officer of the Quartermasters Department at Los Angeles, and in the Southern District of Upper California, an arduous and responsible trust, which he has satisfactorily performed.

3. I regret to report that several most horrible murders have, of late, been committed in this country. The entire occupants of the Mission of San Miguel, men, women and children, in all ten persons were murdered about two weeks ago, and there is no doubt the murders were committed by white men. Murders and robberies have been committed in the mining district, and I am informed that three men were hung in the Pueblo de San Jose, on the 18th inst, for assault with intent to kill. The case is represented to be this – two men were returning from the mines, having about their persons the gold which they had dug amounting, it is said, to 23 pounds. They were met by six men who enquired as usual where they had been working, and with what success: the two men shortly after encamped, and were assaulted; one was shot through the arm, the ball striking the breast, the other begged for mercy and gave up his gold. The six men were later identified and arrested. Only three of the six made the assault, and the evidence against them was so clear, that a jury regularly empaneled, sentenced them to death by hanging. The sentence was executed on Monday last. You are perfectly aware that no competent civil courts exist in this country and that strictly speak-

ing there is no legal power to execute the sentence of death; but the necessity of protecting their lives and property against the many lawless men at large in this country, compels the good citizens to take the law into their own hands. I shall only endeavor to restrain the people so far as to ensure to every man charged with a capital crime, an open and fair trial by a jury of his countrymen.

Upon hearing of the murder of Mr. Reed's family at the Mission of San Miguel, I dispatched Lieut. Ord, with a couple of men to that Mission to ascertain the truth, and if needed to aid the Alcalde, in the execution of his office; as it was reported five men had been found with strong evidence of guilt. I told Lieut. Ord to inform the Alcalde that if the evidence were clear and positive, and the sentence of the jury were death he might cause it to be executed without referring the case to me. This course is absolutely necessary, as there are no jails or prisons in the country where a criminal can be safely secured, their state of affairs must illustrate the absolute necessity of establishing a Territorial Government here as early as practicable, common humanity demands it.

Captain Smith, Lieutenant Davidson and Company C just barely had enough time to settle into the routine of their new garrison at Sonoma when Captain Smith was ordered to San Francisco, on special detached duty. That left Davidson in command of the company and the fort. Since this was his first experience in command he made good use of the opportunity to learn all he could about the responsibilities of the next higher rank. Captain Smith remained away for more than two months, and returned in July. He then assigned Lieutenant Davidson to the task of scouting the entire area, from Sonoma to Sacramento, north to Clear Lake and return. This mission produced valuable information about the habits of the Indians in the area, and an excellent knowledge of the location of their hiding places. A detailed report was given to Captain Smith when

Davidson returned to the fort. After studying the report Captain Smith directed Davidson to organize a large detachment, from Company C, and command an incursion into the region to apprehend all of the hostiles that could be flushed out of hiding. That foray produced nothing in the way of desired results, since the Indians managed to melt into the woods and avoid capture. Follow-up raids were met with the same lack of success, but more valuable knowledge of the Indian activities and habits was gained.

A little later on Captain Smith was ordered away on a short period of detached duty. While he was absent Davidson had a degree of success with one of his missions, as indicated by this excerpt from his report of the event,

> Information having been given me, as commanding officer of the post (Sonoma) that two American citizens had been murdered on their farm at Clear Lake, 70 miles from Sonoma, by the Indians in that vicinity, the company marched on scout on the 26th of December 1849. I returned to the Fort on January 5, 1850. The rainy season and condition of our horses not permitting longer pursuit. Three of the tribe implicated were shot, after being taken prisoners, upon attempting an escape from my camp.

It was not until early May 1850, that another expedition could be sent out from Fort Sonoma for the express purpose of punishing the Indians who had murdered the settlers mentioned in the foregoing excerpt. Lieutenant Davidson in command of Company C, First Dragoons, set out for Clear Lake. En route they were joined by a detachment of infantry commanded by Captain Nathaniel Lyon who, by virtue of his rank, became the commander of the expedition. Davidson had, during the 1849-1850 foray, endeavored to round

up a large group of hostiles in the vicinity of Clear
Lake, but was frustrated in the attempt. Those Indians
were prepared for such an eventuality, and had hidden
canoes along the bank of the lake. When chased by
Davidson they had escaped to an island in the center of
the lake. This time Davidson was prepared for such
tactics by bringing several boats in his supply wagons.
When the Indians were overtaken by the expedition,
they took up previously prepared positions and repulsed
the first charge by the soldiers. The one howitzer, which
accompanied Davidson's detachment, was unlimbered
and poured several shots into the hiding place of the
Indians. They broke out and started pouring a hail of
arrows toward the expeditionary forces, but they were
ineffective. A rapid fire from muskets was returned by
the troops, with deadly effect. Of the Indian force of
some four hundred, more than sixty were slain and the
remainder took to their heels in terror. Some of them
attempted to escape to their island hideaway in the
middle of the lake, but Davidson's men were ready to
intercept them with the boats loaded with Dragoon
riflemen who were stationed at intervals along the shore.
Recognizing the futility of that method of escape the
Indians scattered and melted into the woods. Most of
the Indian survivors managed to get away in that manner. That engagement taught the Indians of the region
to have a healthy respect for the army, which tended to
dampen their interest in raiding American settlements.
The action has been designated, in official records, "The
Action at Clear Lake," on May 15, 1850.

When the operation at Clear Lake was completed the
troops moved on to the Russian River, where two more
settlers, named Stone and Kelly, had been atrociously

murdered by Indians. The culprits were overtaken very near the river and surrounded in a veritable jungle. The troops poured a withering fire into the dense growth and killed seventy-five of the Indians. Once again the remaining Indians, who were terrified, scattered and disappeared in the woods. That occurred on May 17, 1850. A few days later the Dragoons flushed out another large group of hostiles who were encamped on the Sacramento River, near the city of the same name. A bitter battle ensued for a short time, when the Indians realized they were facing certain defeat, and took to their heels. Following this the highly-elated Dragoons returned to Fort Sonoma, extremely proud of the fact that none of their number were killed, and very few suffered minor injuries.

The Dragoons, stationed at Fort Sonoma, continued to play a vital part in maintaining law and order in and around Sacramento, until California became a State on September 9, 1850. At that time the newly established state government enacted a uniform system of laws, and provided for an effective policing operation. As a consequence, the Federal troops were gradually relieved of their police duties. At about the same time that California became a State, Lieutenant Davidson received orders to return to St. Louis, Missouri, for the purpose of recruiting replacements for his regiment. He set out for the east in compliance with orders issued by the local military commander, and arrived in St. Louis before his orders were confirmed by Washington.

3

New Mexico and Apaches

Jefferson Barracks in St. Louis, Lieutenant Davidson's destination, was a recruiting and training depot that provided men for all branches of the army. It was at this location that young men from city streets, farms, ghettos, and elsewhere were transformed into effective soldiers. There were very few of them who had ever used firearms, many were completely undisciplined, and the majority had to learn how to keep themselves clean, especially in the field. Since, at that time, the Dragoons were the elite branch of the army, the pick of the incoming recruits generally wound up in those mounted regiments. Rare, indeed, was there a Dragoon recruit who had knowledge of horses. Therefore, the transformation of a raw recruit into an effective Dragoon presented the training personnel with some exceedingly difficult problems. History has proven, however, that these proud veterans of the saddle did their jobs especially well.

This was a new experience for Davidson, but he plunged into his duties with enthusiasm. He thoroughly enjoyed his work and took keen delight in watching young men, who knew nothing of the military, develop into soldiers proud of their newly acquired abilities and their status as members of an elite corps. Davidson soon became a highly effective training officer utilizing his rich background of combat experience in such a manner that he easily won the respect and admiration of his charges. In addition to the enjoyment of his duty,

Davidson reveled in the luxury of living in reasonably comfortable quarters, and eating three well-prepared meals each day. Certainly a great change from his last four years of rugged living on the frontier, where a blanket under a tree was, often, the best shelter that could be found for the night, and meals consisted of a few beans and dried meat cooked over a campfire, washed down with brackish water. And, of course, another joy for him was in seeing the sights of that great city, St. Louis.

A few weeks after his arrival in St. Louis, Davidson and a friend were walking around in the city, seeing the sights and window shopping. They paused in front of one of the leading portrait studios to look at the display. Prominently featured was the miniature of a young lady which caught the young Lieutenant's eye. She was a lovely girl. Davidson stood looking at the miniature for several minutes as if transfixed, then went into the studio and requested her name from the proprietor who happened to be a most obliging gentleman. Upon rejoining his friend Davidson remarked, "I'm going to marry that girl some day." He next proceeded to make some discreet inquiries, and soon learned that the lady of his choice was the daughter of Mr. George K. McGunnegle, the president of the St. Louis Insurance Company. He also gleaned the knowledge that Miss Clara McGunnegle would be attending a forthcoming reception. It did not take long for the resourceful lieutenant to manipulate an invitation for himself to attend that reception. During the affair it became a simple matter to arrange a formal introduction.[1]

---

[1] The narrative about the meeting, courtship and marriage of John and Clara Davidson is the writer's adaptation of the account given by Clara to her daughters, Elizabeth and Letta.

From the day of the reception young Davidson, in a manner best befitting a dashing Dragoon, literally swept the young lady off her feet. The noisy celebration of ushering in the New Year of 1851 had scarcely ended before Davidson proposed, was accepted, and won her father's consent. The wedding date was set for the middle of the following June. Shortly thereafter he was promoted to the responsible position of Regimental Adjutant. Inasmuch as the regimental headquarters were in Fort Leavenworth, Kansas, it was only a question of time before he would be required to move to that post. The expected move occurred in mid-February, and he joined the headquarters staff late in that same month. This was his first association with the regimental commander of the First Dragoons since General Kearny left that position some years earlier. For the next months the Davidson-McGunnegle romance flourished through the frequent exchange of letters.

It was during her long-range courtship that Clara McGunnegle faced up to some of the realities of army life. She fully realized that her life as an army officer's wife probably would be filled with hardship, something for which the early years had not prepared her. As the daughter of wealthy parents, hers had been a sheltered existence with every possible luxury provided. It was characteristic for the daughters of the wealthy in that era to be thoroughly schooled in the social graces, but they were taught very little of a practical nature. Clara was no exception. The day-to-day problems of managing a household were completely foreign to her, since that was the province of a staff of servants, headed by a competent housekeeper. Clara seldom visited the kitchen, knew nothing about cooking nor menu planning, and, according to family legend, she never wanted for anything because servants were always at her beck and call.

When Clara accepted John Davidson's proposal of marriage she gave no thought to what the future held in store. Her only contact with army personnel was at social functions, therefore she had visualized a somewhat glamorous future as the wife of an army officer. Now, however, she suddenly realized that her first move after the wedding would be to an outpost where the normal comforts of life would be few and far between. She also learned that servants probably would be nonexistent, and that she must learn to do her own meal planning and cooking. Other nerve shattering thoughts crept into her mind, such as the rigors of crossing the plains in wagon trains with the constant menace of hostile Indians. She had often heard stories of these hardships, but gave them little thought until now. When Clara faced up to the problem, her mind dwelt upon her heritage. Her father was an extremely hardy individual who had migrated from Pennsylvania to St. Louis in 1821 at the age of 21. George McGunnegle rode horseback, alone, all the way, and arrived in St. Louis with barely enough money to buy one good meal. Fortunately, however, his uncle happened to be an army officer stationed in the city, who helped young George to find his first job. At that time St. Louis was a land of opportunity for young, hard working and ambitious individuals. George McGunnegle took advantage of every opportunity and within a few years became one of the most prominent and influential residents of the city. He, among others, was instrumental in bringing the first railroad into St. Louis, and then served on its board of directors. With this heritage Clara determined that she had but one course to follow; the wedding would occur as scheduled. She then began to prepare herself to accept all the forthcoming hardships in a manner that would reflect credit upon the name of Davidson.

In early June, with a short leave of absence, Lieutenant Davidson went to St. Louis, where the wedding ceremony took place on June 18, 1851, at the home of his bride's father. The marriage rites were solemnized by Reverend S. G. Gassoway, rector of St. George's Protestant Episcopal Church, the family church. A large number of family friends and relatives attended the wedding and the reception which followed. The newly-weds, however, made their escape as soon as they possibly could for a two-day honeymoon. Lieutenant and Mrs. Davidson then went to Fort Leavenworth, and set up housekeeping in a very small house on the post.

Davidson received orders to join Company I, First Dragoons, in August 1851. The company was then fitting out for a move to New Mexico, while Davidson remained at his post as regimental adjutant awaiting the arrival of the officer designated as his replacement. For some unaccountable reason the new adjutant did not show up on time and Davidson was forced to remain at Fort Leavenworth when Company I started for New Mexico. When the new adjutant did arrive it coincided with the departure of the commander of Company D, on an extended sick leave. Davidson was, therefore, assigned, temporarily, to that company as its commander; an important assignment for such a junior officer. The degree of importance took on added meaning when, a few days later, the company was ordered to proceed, post-haste, to Fort Snelling, Minnesota. The purpose of that hurried move was to strengthen the garrisoned forces in order to put down the uprisings that were being threatened by the Sioux Indians in that general vicinity. Davidson and his new command arrived at Fort Snelling on November 15, 1851, thoroughly tired out after that long, hard march in bitterly cold weather.

Customarily, at that period in our history, the army wives usually accompanied their husbands whenever a force as large as a company was moved to a new post of duty. The women would ride in the wagon trains that carried the supplies and personal belongings of the troops. That move was the first exposure for Clara Davidson to the hardships involved in following her husband from one post of duty to another. Needless to say she lived up to the McGunnegle heritage in every respect. Fortunately there was a cabin available for the Davidsons, and Clara went to work at the task of establishing a new home. Being so far away from the type of civilization that she knew, made her realize that her knowledge of meal planning and preparation was wholly inadequate. She wrote to her father and asked him to send her a good cook book. He replied, "What would you do with one if you had it? You can't even boil water."

But he also sent the book, and the determined young woman made a profound study of that cook book, and learned her lessons well. She mastered the art of cooking and, within a few years, became famous for the excellence of the meals she prepared. She enhanced that reputation by mastering the methods employed by the French, especially the art of wine cookery. According to the information handed down in the family, she was the first wife to introduce French cooking in army circles.

During the months immediately following his arrival in Fort Snelling, the temporary commander of Company D was a very busy man. The fort was situated on a promontory overlooking the Mississippi River, on the outskirts of the town of Minneapolis. The Indians in the surrounding areas were restless and constantly threatening, but no serious outbreaks occurred. It was essential, however, that the Fort Snelling personnel maintain a high degree of vigilance, and have scouting parties on constant patrol in the field. The command of many such patrols provided Davidson with valuable experience that worked to his advantage in the future. He also gained good administrative experience when he succeeded to the temporary command of the fort, during the frequent absences of its regular commander.

Lieutenant Davidson remained at Fort Snelling until September 1852, when the regularly assigned commander of Company D returned from his extended leave of absence, relieving Davidson of his temporary assignment. This afforded an excellent opportunity for a short leave of absence, and the Davidsons took passage on the river boat, for St. Louis. They arrived late in that same month, and were quartered in the McGunnegle home. Exposure to the elements finally caught up with Davidson – he contracted a severe cold which put him on the army sick list. By the time January rolled around Davidson's health had not improved enough to permit him to return to duty, so the local army commander placed him, officially, on sick leave. In that same month the first of the several Davidson children, a daughter, arrived. Although Davidson's health improved considerably, late in January he was continued in sick leave status until May 12, 1853, when he received orders to join to his company in New Mexico. Many days were needed to prepare the family for the long and arduous journey. They were on their way early in June. The records do not indicate exactly how they traveled. There were two modes of transportation between St. Louis and Independence, Missouri, the starting point of the Santa Fe Trail. One was by boat on the Missouri River, and the other by stage coach. Since the river boats provided the best accommodations for ladies it is probable that they traveled in that manner. Upon arrival in Independence several days later it was necessary to await the monthly departure of transportation to Santa Fe. Here again there were two choices – wagon train or stage coach. It is certain that they chose the wagon train since it provided a degree of comfort and safety for the ladies that was not available on stage coaches. The wagon train journey from Independence to Santa Fe took somewhat more than thirty days.

Company I was, at that time, stationed at Cantonment Burgwin, a few miles northeast of Taos, New Mexico. The Davidsons arrived at this post on August 12, 1853. An entry from the diary of Sergeant James A. Bennett, Company I, First Dragoons reads,

> August 12, 1853   Lieut. John Wynn Davidson joined the company. His wife came with him. She is a very beautiful St. Louis lady.

At that time Cantonment Burgwin was one of about twelve forts located along the New Mexican frontier. Distributed among these posts were a total of sixteen hundred and sixty army officers and men, to guard an area containing more than fifty thousand Indians. Of those Indians there were more than twenty thousand Apaches who were actively hostile. The constantly increasing daring of their raids upon settlements, and forays designed to entrap detachments of soldiers in the field, kept the army forces exceedingly busy. Their problem was aggravated by the fact that it was impossible to anticipate those attacks, since the Indians would suddenly appear out of nowhere, make a short attack, then disappear into the surrounding mountains. Long before New Mexico became a territory of the United States, Jacob Sedelmayr, a Catholic Priest, described the Indians as follows,

> The Apaches are exceedingly savage and brutal, and are cruel to those who fall into their hands. They go entirely naked and make their incursions on incredibly swift horses, making the attack with shouts at a great distance in order to strike the enemy with terror. They have not naturally any great share of courage, and in war they rather depend on artifice than valor. If defeated they will submit to the most ignominious terms, and will keep their treaties no longer than suits their convenience.

Early in March 1854 a Mrs. White was brutally ravished by a Jicarilla Apache named Lobo Blanco. A detachment of Dragoons commanded by Lieutenant Bell was sent out to punish the guilty parties. They caught up with Lobo Blanco and his band of Indians, and a short battle ensued in which Lobo was killed. Shortly thereafter Lieutenant Bell's detachment was attacked by an overwhelmingly superior band of Jicarillas and given a severe beating. Upon notification of that encounter Major George A. Blake, commander of Cantonment Burgwin, ordered Lieutenant Davidson to organize a detachment of Dragoons and take to the field, "to watch and restrain" the Apache warriors. Their immediate objective was to flush out a partic-

ularly troublesome band of Indians that was expected
to be encamped in the nearby foothills. Davidson rode
out of the post at the head of a sixty-man detachment
and headed down the road toward Taos. They did not
locate the expected band in the foothills, so continued
through Taos and headed for the Embudo mountains.
At a point about twenty miles south of Taos, as they
entered the mountains, they were ambushed in a rocky
defile by a force of more than two hundred and fifty
Jicarilla Apaches. Obviously the Indians had chosen
their point of attack with great care.

At a prearranged signal the Indians swooped down
upon the Dragoons, catching them unaware. There was
no retreat for the Dragoons for they were boxed in on
all sides. The Dragoons rallied and launched a counter-
attack, but it was unsuccessful because their horses could
not scale the steep sides of the ravine. The troopers dismounted and charged on foot, advancing up the mountain sides, in the face of a withering fire, and drove the
Apaches from their positions. The Indians hastily retreated to higher ground, then regrouped and waited
for the Dragoons. When the troopers clawed their way
up the sides of the ravine and were within range, the
Indians again met the attack with bursts of heavy fire,
then retreated. These tactics were repeated several
times, and each time the Indians fell back they would
be joined by others who were waiting in the hills. As a
consequence the Indians grew stronger with each attack, while the Dragoons were weakened by their losses.
These losses eventually reached a point where Davidson
was forced to withdraw. That he did, under constant
hit-and-run tactics by rapidly growing numbers of Indians. The Dragoons, however, met each of the Indian

charges by wheeling and counter-attacking with such telling effect that the Indians were too intimidated to attempt a full scale attack. In that manner the troopers finally fought their way to the relative safety of the main road to Taos, then on to Cantonment Burgwin.

That ambush occurred on March 30, 1854, and is officially in the army records of engagements as "The Action of Cieneguilla." In the action twenty Dragoons were killed, and every man and officer wounded, some seriously. The army high command in New Mexico considered the operation to be a success in spite of the heavy losses, because it caused the Indians to flee across the Del Norte River. Kit Carson, who was then the Indian Agent at Taos, visited the scene of the action on March 31, and, through observation and inquiries, acquired an accurate account of the battle. He stated that it was "one of the most desperate fights in our Indian record." His description of it is as follows,

The Dragoons dismounted, clambered up the steep sides of the canyon to dislodge the shrieking reds, but only scattered them among the rocks. The Apaches, light of foot and shifty of movement, outnumbering the belted soldiers four to one, took steady toll with shaft and lead. The Dragoons' horses, left below under guard, were endangered. Cheered again and again by Davidson [in threatened disaster "as cool and collected as if under the guns of his fort" it was reported to Carson] the soldiers cut their way back. Just in time they reached their saddle stock. Retreat was sounded. This brought on a closer set-to, of saber and pistol against lance and arrow. . .

I know Davidson well, having been in engagements when he done a prominent part and I know him to be as brave as an officer can be, and from the men that were in the engagement of that day I have been informed that during the fight he never took ambush and that when in retreat, he directed his men to take shelter as best they could, but that he, fearing no danger, remained exposed to the fire of the Indians.

The commander of Cantonment Burgwin, Major Blake, upon learning of the fight from Davidson, immediately dispatched a full report of that engagement to Brigadier General John Garland, Commander Army Headquarters, Albuquerque, New Mexico. The General, in turn, ordered Lieutenant Colonel Philip St. George Cooke, Commander Fort Union, New Mexico, "to proceed forthwith to Don Fernando de Taos with such force as can be spared from Fort Union, and take charge of operations." [2]

The General, next, sent a full report to Army Headquarters in Washington. By this time he had the report of the action, as submitted by Kit Carson. The general's report, dated April 1, 1854, included the following remarks, [3]

> The Indians, Jicarillas Apaches and Utahs, have managed to combine a force of 250 warriors and unexpectedly attacked a company of Dragoons 60 strong, about 25 miles from Fernandez de Taos, under the command of Lieutenant Davidson, First Dragoons, and succeeded, after a desperate conflict, in overwhelming it. Lieut. Davidson and Assistant Surgeon Magruder, both wounded, returned from the battlefield with about seventeen men, most of them wounded. The troops displayed a gallantry seldom equalled in this or any other country, and the officer in command, Lieut. Davidson, has given evidence of soldiership in the highest degree creditable to him. To have sustained a deadly contest of three hours, when he was so greatly outnumbered, and to have returned with the fragment of a company crippled up, is amazing and calls for the admiration of every true soldier. To prevent further disaster, I have ordered Lieut. Col. Cooke, Second Dragoons, to take the field with about 200 Dragoons and a company of artillery armed with rifles.

---

2 Department of New Mexico Orders, vol. 9, P, 152. NA, RG 98.

3 John W. Davidson Appointment, Commission, and Personal file, National Archives, Washington, D.C. (hereafter cited as ACP file).

When General Garland's orders reached Fort Union, Lieutenant Colonel Cooke departed without delay. The timing of Cooke's departure is a moot point among historians, since Cooke claims, in his memoirs, to have left Fort Union on the mission prior to the receipt of any orders to do so. This writer chooses to believe that Cooke's departure occurred as a result of the General's orders. It is a matter of the credibility of Cooke's memoirs, as will be discussed later. At any rate Cooke's force chased the offending Indians until they were overtaken at Aguas Calientes, and given a sound thrashing. This gained for Cooke an excellent reputation as an Indian fighter, which probably was deserved.

Without intending to detract from the excellence of Cooke's performance during the Aguas Calientes action, it is interesting to note his uncomplimentary discussion of the "Action of Cieneguilla" in his memoirs. According to Cooke,

> Davidson was thirsting for revenge for the severe beating suffered by Lieut. Bell, and hastily assembled a detachment to hunt down the offending Indians, and rashly plunged into a trap.

Cooke completely ignores the fact that Davidson acted in response to a lawful order from his commanding officer, Major Blake. He also chooses to ignore the fact that no mere lieutenant could, or would, lead a detachment out of a post without the sanction of the commander of that post. As for rashly plunging into a trap, Kit Carson, one of the greatest Indian fighters who ever lived, stated in his memoirs, "The trap had long been prepared by the Indians, it was unknown to the military, and no one could have avoided it."

It was a well-known fact, throughout the army in the

far west, that Lieutenant Colonel Cooke had a trigger-quick temper, often flared up over trivialities, and soundly berated subordinates before he had possession of all relevant facts. Kit Carson touches upon this in his memoirs, then concludes his reference to Cooke with the following remarks,

> He was a character of renown in western army memories as a very peppery man with language, who talked through his nose so that you could hardly understand him, *but,* you had to understand him. . . As efficient an officer to make campaigns against Indians as I ever accompanied; that he is brave and gallant all know.

Brave, gallant and competent as Cooke was as an Indian fighter, he could not hold his own during the Civil War. He was breveted a major general and assigned to several important field commands. In each case he failed to complete the assigned mission in a creditable manner. As a result the army high command transferred Cooke to relatively unimportant posts, far from all combat operations (in military parlance, he was placed on the shelf).

Evidently Cooke's failure in the theater of war, and the subsequent shelving, preyed upon his mind and probably generated a feeling of bitterness. It was during that period of his life that he wrote his memoirs. While Cooke was failing on the field of battle, Davidson, also a general officer, was establishing a fine reputation as a cavalry commander. In short, Cooke's star was declining while Davidson's was ascending. Could it be, therefore, that Cooke's uncomplimentary remarks about Davidson's performance in the "Action of Cieneguilla" were prompted by both bitterness and jealousy?

For a short time following Cooke's successful sweep

against the Apaches, relative quiet prevailed in the vicinity of Cantonment Burgwin. But early in May the hostiles became especially troublesome. General Garland had no choice but to order a large force, commanded by Major Carleton of the First Dragoons, into the field to track down a large band of the hostile Jicarillas. The force, including Company I, First Dragoons, with Lieutenant Davidson in command, departed from Taos on May 23, 1854, and followed a northerly course. They scouted to the north through the mountains, then turned east between "East and West Spanish Peaks," and picked up the trail of the Indians near Raton Pass. The course followed by Major Carleton led directly up Fisher's Peak, and when he reached the mesa on top the Indians were located in a camp below. Each of the three company commanders led his troops in a charge, from different directions, and put the Indians to rout. Most of them escaped, but without their horses. The major then decided that enough punishment had been meted out to the Apaches, and withdrew his force to start marching back to Taos, through Raton Pass. They arrived on June 12, 1854.

However, the Indians in the general vicinity of Taos had not learned their lesson, and became increasingly troublesome. That necessitated much greater vigilance, and more troops patrolling in the field than ever before. Davidson had a full share of these activities and was involved in numerous sharp skirmishes with the Apaches. One large scale mission, for scouting the entire area, was organized by General Garland. Three separate detachments were involved and took to the field on October 2, 1854. One detachment of fifty men, under Major Carleton of the First Dragoons, was directed to scout as far south as Bosque Redondo (later Fort Sumner), then up the Pecos River to Anton Chico. Another such detachment was Company I, commanded by Lieutenant Davidson, directed to scout the Pecos River area from Anton Chico to the north. The third group, under Major Thompson, Second Dragoons, was assigned to scout east to a point on the north side of the Red River near the Santa Fe Trail, and endeavor to maintain contact with Davidson. The twofold purpose of the mission, as directed by General Garland, was to flush out roving bands of hostile Apaches, and to locate suitable sites for military posts. Davidson did flush out a band of Apaches that had been raiding the settlers in San Miguel County, and punished them in a sharp skirmish. The other detachments had similar experiences. Some of the locations selected by the detachments became military posts at later dates.

The ushering in of the New Year, 1855, brought some especially good news for the Davidsons. In January notification arrived that the lieutenant would henceforth be a captain. Almost ten years out of West Point, and Davidson was beginning to wonder if he ever would reach the next higher grade. The promotion to captain was effective January 20, 1855, and it brought his first official Company Command. All such previous commands had been on a temporary basis. He was ordered to take command of Company B, First Dragoons, then located at Fort Fillmore, New Mexico. The fort was situated on the Rio Grande, about forty miles north of the Texas border. It was one of the more important posts in the expanding chain of forts along the territorial frontier, commanded by Lieutenant Colonel Dixon Miles of the Third Infantry. When the Davidsons arrived in mid-March, they were warmly welcomed by the officers' wives of the garrison. The next few weeks were busy ones for Davidson for, in addition to all the courtesy calls to be made, he must become acquainted with the officers and men of his new command. Then, too, were the problems of that locality that must be studied. Within a short time after Davidson's arrival Colonel Miles received instructions to construct a new fort in the Capitan Mountains, about two hundred miles northeast of Fort Fillmore. Miles, in turn, designated Davidson as his chief assistant for superintending the projects. As would be expected, Davidson and his Company B became the first occupants of the new post when it was completed. The post was officially designated Fort Stanton on June 20, 1855, and the company of Dragoons moved in.

A few weeks after Captain Davidson moved Company B into Fort Stanton, he received a new and interesting assignment. He was directed to organize and command an expedition to march to the mouth of Delaware Creek, at its junction with the Pecos River, for the purpose of opening a new route of communications between that point and Fort Stanton. Evidently this was in conjunction with a survey being made by Captain Pope, U.S. Army, that would establish a route for the Pacific Railway. Pope had started from the railroad's projected terminal in eastern Texas, with the ultimate destination being San Diego. That survey was in accordance with the 1854 Congressional authorization of explorations for routes for a railroad to the Pacific.[4] Shortly before Davidson's departure preparations were completed, information was received that

---

[4] 33 Cong., 2 sess., *House Exec. Doc. no. 91.*

Capain Pope was hemmed in by hostile Comanche Indians at his camp on the Rio Pecos, and had already lost seven men. Davidson expedited his preparations and started out from Fort Stanton on August 21, 1855.

The route followed from Fort Stanton, according to the best available records, was down the Rio Bonita to the Rio Ruidoso, thence overland to the Rio Pecos, where they arrived on August 24. The ground they covered after leaving the Rio Ruidoso, has been described as full of vermin, abounding with rattlesnakes, centipedes and tarantulas running all over the ground. Traveling down the Pecos they crossed the Rio Penasco at its mouth, then at "Blue Water" the depth was such that they had to swim the horses across and float the supply wagons. From that time onward the daytime temperature ran above 121 degrees, causing both men and animals to suffer extreme discomfort, especially because the Pecos River water was brackish and unpalatable.

The expedition arrived at Captain Pope's camp on September 1, 1855. Under Pope's command were seventy-six men of Company I, Seventh Infantry, and eighty civilians. Davidson found them to be busily engaged in drilling artesian wells on the Llano Estacado (Staked Plain), one of which had reached a depth of eight hundred feet, without striking water. (This later became known as Pope's Well and is shown on the old maps of the region. It disappeared many years later when a dam was built on the Pecos River to form Red Bluff Lake.) The Dragoons learned that the reported Indian menace was a false alarm and, after a few days' rest, they continued down the Pecos to the mouth of Delaware Creek. A totally different route was followed on the return trip to Fort Stanton. It was carefully mapped, and described as superior to, and shorter than, the one used on the outbound leg. They arrived back in Fort Stanton on September 16, 1855. Davidson's detailed report, together with complete maps, charts, topographical data, and other important information was submitted to General Garland on June 17, 1856. The total distance covered on that expedition was in excess of two hundred miles outbound, and one hundred and seventy miles return.

Company B had very little time to rest up from their difficult expedition to the Pecos. In October orders were received to prepare for a return to Fort Fillmore, and they made the move towards the end of the same month. In January 1856, Captain Davidson received orders to report to the headquarters of the Army Territorial Command, in order to appear before a Court of Inquiry in regard to his conduct during the "Action of Cieneguilla." (It is interesting to note how slowly the army acted to investigate the circumstances of that tragic affair, in which more than twenty men lost their lives.) Davidson arrived at headquarters about the first of February 1856. The court convened on February 4, 1856, and closed on the seventh in the late afternoon. During the hearing Davidson was questioned very closely, as were Lieutenant Robert Williams and Sergeant Bennett of the First Dragoons who were participants in the battle, and Kit Carson. Sergeant Bennett was severely wounded during the battle and nearly lost his life. Kit Carson was filling the role of expert witness. When the court closed and its findings were submitted, Davidson's conduct during the action was adjudged to be "completely blameless."

On February 24 Davidson led a detachment of eighty men from Fort Fillmore, and headed for the Organ Mountains in search of a band of Indians who had stolen a drummer boy from Fort Bliss, Texas. Fort Bliss was located about fifty miles south of Fort Fillmore. The detachment met with the Indians at the mouth of Bog Canyon, and Davidson talked with the chiefs. The Indians insisted they had no knowledge of the drummer boy, but would endeavor to find and bring him to Fort Fillmore. While returning to its home base the detachment captured an Indian squaw and questioned her about the boy. She stated that the boy had not been able to keep up with the Indians, and had died from the severe beatings inflicted by his captors. This was but one of the many instances of the cruel and inhuman treatment of captives by the Apaches. The detachment returned to Fort Fillmore on March 3, and Davidson was greeted by orders to move his company back to Fort Stanton. They started out the next day and arrived at their destination about a week later. For the next several months there was little activity in the field, and these tired troopers had an opportunity to rest and refurbish their equipment.

The arrival of that year, 1856, seemed to be the signal for the introduction of a multitude of additional responsibilities for the already overloaded military establishment in New Mexico. When the War with Mexico ended, all the territory north of the Gila River was ceded to the United States, and the army assumed responsibility for maintaining the peace. As previously mentioned, some 1500 soldiers faced a hostile force of Indians amounting to 20,000 or more. The Gadsden purchase of 1853, which was ratified by the Mexican and

United States governments much later, added all of the
area between the Gila River and the Mexican border to
the Territory of New Mexico. This also added over five
thousand exceedingly hostile Indians to the already-
troublesome Apache population of the territory. But –
the army strength was not increased one bit. As one
measure, to control the situation, several new posts were
added in strategic locations. One of the new posts was
Camp Moore, established in mid-1856, which became
Fort Buchanan in June 1857. It was situated near the
town of Sonoita, just a few miles north of the Mexican
border town of Nogales. Its mission was to protect the
Santa Cruz Valley, and to keep a check on the Indians
from there to the Gila River. The post would be garrisoned by four Companies of the First Dragoons, including Company B.

Captain Davidson led Company B out of Fort Stanton in July 1856, with instructions to scout a large area
of the territory while en route to his new post in the
Santa Cruz Mountains. For the next eleven months
Company B was almost constantly in the field on scouting activities. The log of their campsites suggests that,
during that period, they covered most of the southern
part of the Territory of New Mexico. With each
monthly report of their activities, the camp locations
were given as follows: August, vicinity of Fort Craig;
September, vicinity of Fort Thorn; October, on the Rio
San Simon; November, near the Calabasas Ranch; January, vicinity of Camp Moore, and camped in the Santa
Cruz Mountains; February, Camp Ojo Caliente;
March, vicinity of Camp Moore; April, Camp Moore;
May, camped at Mount Graham; June and July,
camped on the Rio San Carlos. They finally arrived at

their destination, Fort Buchanan (as it had been designated in June), in August 1857.

Company B, which had experienced nearly one year
of rigorous field service, had been looking forward to
the comforts normally provided by a garrison. Their
dismay at what they saw upon arrival in Fort Buchanan
is indescribable, and probably unleashed some exceedingly strong expressions that were far from compli-
mentary. That fort was situated in the worst area of all
the army posts in what was then New Mexico, and was
"blessed" with the poorest building construction that
can be imagined. The post consisted of a series of ugly,
shack-like buildings that were completely lacking in
comfort. Living quarters were constructed of upright
posts of decaying timber, and plastered with adobe
mud. Flat roofs and floors were covered with dirt and
grass, and the rooms were low, narrow and without
ventilation. The stables, corrals, pig pens and living
quarters were scattered over a distance of half a mile.
The garrisoned troops suffered constantly because of
the unusually unhealthy location. In spite of these hardships and forbidding circumstances, the families accompanied the soldiers to Fort Buchanan.

For years the Mimbres, Gila and Coyotero bands of
Apaches had terrorized the frontier settlements west of
the Rio Grande, and on both sides of the border. Their
bold forays extended far to the north in which they
stole cattle, attacked settlements frequently, and often
escaped across the border where the United States
troops were not supposed to go. One wonders just how
scrupulous they were about that restriction. That section of the Territory was filled with mountains, ravines,
huge rocks, and forests of Saguaro cactus, all of which

afforded excellent cover for the Indians who knew every foot of the ground. The pitifully small number of soldiers who were stationed in the area were hard pressed to protect the miners and settlers, who moved into the territory in ever increasing numbers. Although some of the tribes were peaceful, Mexican bandits often crossed the border and endeavored to create trouble among them. The bandits nearly succeeded in early 1858 when they attacked peaceful tribes near Albuquerque, and caused the Pinal Apaches to go on the rampage.

Because of these highly unsettled conditions the troops at Fort Buchanan were kept exceedingly busy on scouting expeditions in the field. The term "scouting expeditions" was used in all official reports to describe the activities of the numerous detachments who were always in the field, hunting down roving bands of hostile Indians. One such occurred between February 15 and March 8, 1858, when the Pinal Apaches flared up. Captain Davidson commanded a detachment of seventy men, and marched into the Pinal country to patrol along the banks of the Gila River. It was intended as a surprise attack, but the surprise element failed because the Indians had the peculiar ability to observe without being observed. However, it was reported that this detachment did gain valuable new knowledge about the character of the country, and the strength of the Indians of the area. Later reports indicated that the value of the knowledge gained was most helpful for operating subsequent scouting expeditions.

When one considers the unhealthy locale and the innumerable hardships involved in just plain living at Fort Buchanan, it is a great tribute to the fortitude of the women who followed their army husbands to such outposts. Far from their accustomed civilization they had to improvise and create homes from dirt-floored shacks that were hardly fit for human habitation. Social activities revolved around the few families that populated the posts. Adding to the difficulties of living within the boundaries of Fort Buchanan was its isolation from a population center of any consequence. They managed to offset some of the boredom by organizing parties, dances, picnics and games. Then there were occasional visits to Tucson, some fifty miles to the north, when the husbands could arrange for short leaves of absence. Medical and nursing services were limited to the post surgeon, while the wives provided whatever nursing might be needed. It was into this environment that Mrs. Clara Davidson presented her husband with a new son (the father of this writer) on February 1, 1858. The baby was christened George Kennedy Davidson in honor of his grandfather, George Kennedy McGunnegle. That event swelled the size of the Davidson household to three children, two of whom were of school age. It was the mother's lot to supervise the education of these children, with the guidance and assistance of the post chaplain. It was far from a dull existence for that lady.

4

Again to California

In the early part of the year 1858, shortly after the birth of his new son, Captain Davidson received word of another change of duty. Information of the change arrived before the actual receipt of orders, and it met with the unanimous approval of the entire family. It promised a decided improvement over the generally unpleasant living conditions they had endured in that undeveloped region along the Mexican border. Davidson was probably chosen for the operation because of his intimate knowledge of California, and the route thereto. In accordance with Department of New Mexico Orders No. 3, of April 3, 1858, transmitting General Order No. 5, of January 2, 1858, he was directed to command a movement of troops from Fort Buchanan to the Department of Pacific. This movement of troops included Companies B and K of the First Dragoons, and a large number of recruits that were en route from Jefferson Barracks, Missouri, to Fort Tejon. The size of this expedition necessitated the use of numerous equipment, commissary, baggage and passenger wagons. Consequently dependents accompanied the expedition.

Captain Davidson led the expedition out of Fort Buchanan on May 12, 1858, and headed for California, with the first stop designated as Fort Yuma on the California side of the Colorado River. Upon arrival at that point they paused for a very few days to rest, then moved on. In order to avoid the blistering desert lying

to the west of Yuma, Davidson headed north along the
Colorado to a point approximating the present city of
Blythe, California. At that point they turned due west,
toward San Bernardino, California. Although the
march had been arduous they were fortunate in not
being molested by hostile Indians, and made good time.
The expedition reached San Bernardino on Saturday,
June 12, 1858, and encamped for several days in order
to give personnel and animals an opportunity to recuperate from the rigorous march across the mountains.
The arrival of this force at Fort Tejon occurred on
Tuesday, July 16, 1858. Davidson and his family settled
into the quarters allotted to them, and found themselves
far more comfortably situated than at any time since
their marriage six years earlier. The garrison life in the
Fort was enjoyable, and the mild climate provided a
pleasant relief from the arid deserts of New Mexico.

Since Fort Tejon had been established for the purpose of protecting settlers from bands of marauding
Indians, and the numerous bandits who roamed throughout the area, the Dragoons were kept busy, which gave
Davidson many opportunities to become familiar with
the countryside as he led scouting patrols into the field.
One such foray began on September 22, 1858 when a
detachment of forty-one Dragoons, commanded by
Captain Davidson, left the fort and headed for San
Bernardino and the headwaters of the Mojave River,
to track down and subdue a large party of hostile Indians that was reported to be in that area. They reached
San Bernardino and scouted the surrounding territory,
then worked their way through the mountains to the
west. The entire region was covered with the greatest of
care but no Indians were located. Six weeks later, on

November 7, they returned to the fort wet, cold and thoroughly disgusted with the results attained.

The following April (1859) Major James H. Carleton, First Dragoons, received orders from the commanding general, Department of Pacific, to escort the United States paymaster, Major Henry Prince, to Salt Lake City. He was further instructed that, while en route, he should investigate the massacre that had occurred at Mountain Meadows, Utah Territory, in September 1857. Due to the reports of large scale Indian uprisings in the territory he was directed to assemble a force of two plus companies of Dragoons, to chase down and administer appropriate punishment to the offenders. The two companies were Company K, commanded by Carleton, and Company I, commanded by Captain Davidson. The expedition set out within a matter of days after receipt of their orders, and followed a route that approximates the present day highway from Los Angeles to Salt Lake City, via Las Vegas. All along the way they picked up tales of the way Indians had been making life miserable for settlers.

Upon arrival in Mountain Meadows it was learned that, contrary to popular opinion, the Indians were not wholly responsible for the massacre. Briefly, the incident probably occurred because of Mormon resentment of their earlier persecutions and the murder of their Orson Pratt in Arkansas, as well as the fear of the United States Army force approaching Utah at that time, and various irritations arising as the emigrants were traversing Utah. Consequently, when the emigrants, known as the Fancher Party of some 120 persons, camped at Mountain Meadows, a force of about fifty Mormons and numerous Indians set upon them and slaughtered the entire party except for a few small children. And to make bad matters worse the victims were not even buried. As reported by Carleton, he had never seen a worse crime. Since more than a year had elapsed since the massacre there were few bones left, which were buried by Carleton's force, with appropriate ceremony. A monument was also erected to commemorate the tragedy. The Indians, well aware of Carleton's mission, had completely dispersed and disappeared into the surrounding mountains. Therefore, the paymaster was sent on to Salt Lake City, and Carleton's expedition started the return journey to Fort Tejon, where they arrived in early June. The route of the expedition, going and coming, was mapped in detail by Captain Davidson.

Davidson did not have long to rest from that trip. He was selected for an unusually important project. It was to organize and command an expedition to Owens Lake and the Owens River to recover stock that had been reported as stolen by the Indians in that area. His orders were: first, recover the stock and mete out appropriate punishment to the guilty parties; second, develop a detailed map of the surrounding country. Extensive preparations were necessary, since surveying, mapping and other special instruments would be needed, as well as civilian technicians. On July 21, 1859, the expedition set out with Captain Davidson in command, assisted by Lieutenant Chapman. The operation may best be described by the following excerpt from the Los Angeles Star, edition dated Saturday, August 27, 1859:

> In consequence of the extensive depredations committed in the San Fernando Valley, Lt. Col. Beall, Commanding Fort Tejon, sent a detachment of First Dragoons, under command of Cap-

tain Davidson, to explore the Indian country. Captain Davidson made a map of the explorations and discovered a pass through the mountains to Salt Lake road, which will shorten the distance to Salt Lake and avoid the journey over the Desert, besides opening up a route on which wood, water and grass are abundant.

Captain Davidson, being under military publicity restrictions, could not discuss the expedition further than to assure that the Owen's Lake Indians were quiet, industrious and reliable. However, through the kindness of a civilian who accompanied the expedition, a very interesting letter from him is published.

"Tejon, August, 1859. The selected route of Captain Davidson's expedition was through Walker's Basin and the Kern River mines; up the south fork of the Kern River to Walker's Pass, then along the eastern slope of the Sierra Nevada to Owen's Lake. The Distance from Fort Tejon to the Desert via Walker's pass is about 117 miles. Arriving at the foot of the Lake a fine meadow of 800 to 1000 acres with good water was found. But it is the only desirable spot in the vicinity because the Lake is saline.

Large tracts of ground some 27 miles above and 62 miles east of the Lake were found to be irrigated by the Natives, in order to grow a small tuberous root with excellent nutritious properties, which is one of the mainstays of their diet. The irrigation ditches are many miles long and are laid out as if they had been plotted by an engineer, and were dug without the aid of agricultural implements.

To our surprise we saw very few horses. The Indians informed Captain Davidson that, some five years ago several of the Indians were in the habit of stealing horses for the purpose of eating them. This was deemed sinful by the elders of the Tribe, so they were punished with death.

While talking to the Wokopee Indian's Head Men, Captain Davidson informed them that the U.S. Government would protect them as long as they were peaceful. The Indians readily agreed to cooperate.

The untiring energy and industry exhibited by Captain Davidson in carrying out his instructions is certainly worthy of all commendation; and if courteous and gentlemanly conduct towards those who accompanied the expedition, and untiring attention to, and solicitude for, the well being and comfort of the soldiers of the command, be marks of the true soldier, then the First Dragoons may well be proud of the officers of this command.

Of great and permanent importance to the country is the labors of Captain Davidson in establishing a direct route between Salt Lake and all parts of California, avoiding entirely the Mojave Desert, and securing a good and direct road with plenty of water and grass at proper distances. Captain Davidson said that this can be done by carrying a road along the rim of the Great Basin, and entering the Wokopee, or Owen's Valley at it's head by a very excellent Pass.   Signed: QUIS"

The total distance covered on that expedition, in both directions, was slightly over 638 miles. The exact route followed is not available, even in National Archives. But a reading of Davidson's report to the commander, Fort Tejon, dated August 21, 1859, indicates a march from the fort to a spot near the present city of Bakersfield, then to the South Fork of the Kern River. That river was followed to Walker's Pass, then on to Owens Lake, now dry. The new Salt Lake City route probably would be to go on north to Big Pine, thence veering eastward towards that city, thus passing to the north of Death Valley. The return trip followed the same route, except that a direct march was made from Walker's Pass back to Fort Tejon.

An interesting sidelight to Captain Davidson's activities at Fort Tejon is the introduction of the "Camel Corps" to the post. Shortly after taking command of the fort, Lieutenant Colonel Beale, and others in Washington, conceived the idea of using camels as beasts of burden in that section of California. It was their thought that camels would readily adapt to the prevailing climate, and be especially valuable for the long stretches of desert where watering places were few and far between. Although the experiment did not produce the hoped-for results, the Dragoons at the fort acquired an excellent knowledge of the idiosyncrasies of that particular species of animal. Captain Davidson came in for a full measure of experience with the Camel Corps, and thus became one of the very few army officers experienced with the use of horses, mules, and camels.

The latter part of 1859 and early 1860 were relatively quiet in the general vicinity of Fort Tejon, and scouting missions dwindled down to almost nothing. In the spring of 1860, however, the picture changed for Davidson. He received the assignment to return east to pick up another large contingent of recruits, and bring them to California. He met the recruits in New Mexico, near Santa Fe, and marched them across a route far to the north of any previously used. The entire trip turned out to be purely routine, with no unusual incidents of any kind. Upon his return to Fort Tejon, Davidson was assigned to the post of regimental quartermaster, which turned out to be most enjoyable because it enabled him to spend more time with his family than ever before.

In the latter part of 1860 a question arose regarding the desirability of maintaining Fort Tejon as an active military post. It seems that arguments, both pro and con, were being advanced by the settlers in the area and by many of the higher ranking military personnel. In order to obtain an unbiased military study of the entire situation the commanding general, Brigadier General Albert Sidney Johnston, assigned Captain Davidson to make an extensive survey of the entire situation, and submit his findings and recommendation. For the next two months Davidson made an on-the-spot study of all conceivable alternatives. Upon the conclusion of this effort he drafted a lengthy report pointing up the advantages and disadvantages of the various possibilities, then recommended closing the fort with the following statement,

> The annual cost, to the Government, of maintaining the Fort is about $55,000.00 more than it would cost to maintain a similar post in San Bernardino, or Los Angeles. As matters now stand the Fort is virtually useless, and offers no protection whatever for white settlements as it can easily be by-passed by savages and bandits. Furthermore, it is located in a cold, bleak, inhospitable, and worthless region that is rocked by earthquakes. It is unsuitable for habitation of white men, and is deserted by the Indians.

It is entirely possible that Davidson and Lieutenant Colonel Beale clashed over his recommendation for closing the fort. Beale was one of those who had argued for its retention, probably because it was to his personal advantage that the fort continue in operation. During his tenure as post commander, Beale had been buying property in the vicinity of Fort Tejon. At any rate, the reaction to Davidson's report was not long in coming, and it was decided to phase out Fort Tejon as an active military post. One of the first moves was the establishment of a post in Los Angeles, called Camp Fitzgerald, with Major Carleton in command. The site of that camp was in an area that is now downtown Los Angeles, on Broadway between First and Second streets. On June 19, 1861, Company B, First Dragoons, commanded by Captain Davidson was moved into the new camp. Within the next month the entire garrison had vacated Fort Tejon, and dispersed to several different locations in the state. Fort Tejon remained in an inactive status until it was re-opened in 1863. It closed its gates for the last time on September 11, 1864, and was abandoned by the army.

Within a matter of days after Davidson settled into Camp Fitzgerald, Major Carleton received a new assignment and Captain Davidson became commanding officer of the post. By this time the Civil War was in full swing in the East. When news of the conflict reached California the entire population, including the military, began choosing up sides. As a result, many of those who had been closely associated in the past now found themselves on opposite sides of the fence, and, in many cases, these differences brought on serious confrontations. The commanding general of the Pacific, Bragidier General Albert Sidney Johnston, a native of Kentucky, decided to resign his commission to join the Confederate Army. In full justice to the general, he insisted upon complete loyalty to the Union, from all subordinates and himself, for as long as they remained soldiers in the United States Army. One day, after General Johnston had made his decision, he made a personal call upon Captain Davidson. Davidson felt complimented, as well as pleased, to receive the general in his office, which was a reversal of the usual procedure. And, it might be added, Davidson had a very high regard for General Johnston.

The meeting was on a very friendly basis, during which the general outlined his reasons for leaving the United States Army, then stated that he had just resigned his commission to accept a commission as major general in the Confederate Army. He then endeavored to recruit Davidson for the Army of the South. Johnston was an exceptionally articulate and persuasive individual. He appealed to Davidson's birthright as a Virginian, who had deep roots in the South, and was steeped in southern customs and traditions. Certainly, according to Johnston, Davidson should be loyal to his homeland, and, of course, his father and mother were buried in that state. Then, of course, there was the ancestral home in Vienna, Virginia, just a few miles from Washington, D.C. As the conversation progressed it was brought out that Davidson's younger brothers, Roger and Charles, probably would join the Confederates. Two other relatives in the United States Navy service, his uncle, Commander Thomas Hunter, was almost certain to go with the South, and, quite possibly, his other brother, Lieutenant Hunter Davidson, might do the same. As it turned out Hunter Davidson did resign, after eighteen years of service, to join the Confederate Navy as a lieutenant. The others ultimately did take up arms for the Confederate States. Sensing all the conflicting thoughts that ran through Davidson's mind, General Johnston voiced the most powerful argument that could be used in such a situation. He said, "Davidson, you must come with us; you belong in our Army, and we'll make you a General." [1]

Davidson was stunned by the magnitude of the offer of a general's stars, for it was beyond his wildest dreams to ever attain the rank of general. For one who is not familiar with the army in the years prior to the Civil War, it would be almost impossible to realize the impact of such an offer. Promotions in the army were agonizingly slow; Davidson was only a captain after serving for sixteen years since graduation from West Point. He readily visualized the financial improvement, and the host of other advantages that accompanied the rank of general. His thoughts also ran

---

[1] 49 Cong., 1 sess., *Senate Rept. 1306* (June 10, 1886); and *House Rept. 2943* (June 22, 1886).　　　　[2] *Ibid.*

through the many years of hardship duty in outposts, which involved frequent clashes with enemy forces. Through it all his family had accompanied him without complaint. He well knew that the rank of general would include the provision of comfortable quarters for his dependents, as well as other prerequisites for himself that were not now enjoyed.

Another item that one would find difficult to appreciate, if not reared in the Southern States, is the tremendous pressures that were brought to bear on officers of southern extraction. The South was exceedingly anxious to recruit competent leaders for the Confederate military, and that the recruiters were successful, in many cases, has been proven by the events of history. The moral strength displayed by those men who resisted the pressure, would also be difficult to appreciate. Davidson thought deeply about all the points discussed, for a period of several minutes. Finally he replied to the General by saying, "Oh no, General, I'll stand by the Flag that I promised to protect." [2] That resolute statement had no doubtful sound, no uncertain meaning. He had firmly cast his lot, without reservation, with the Union of the States as a Nation.

As an introspective sidelight, it is interesting to note that when the Civil War broke out, army and navy officers were at liberty to resign their commissions. Out of a total of 1036 army officers 286 resigned; of the navy's 1300 officers 322 resigned. In the process the South acquired some of the Union's finest officers. At the time General Winfield Scott, General-in-Chief of the United States Army, who was a Virginian, was expected to go with the South, but he did not.

Soon after refusing General Johnston's offer, Davidson's problems, as commander of Camp Fitzgerald, increased rapidly. The divided citizenry of Los Angeles were constantly brawling, and on the verge of open warfare. Much of the turmoil resulted from the pressures being applied by the Confederates, to the local residents, in an effort to gain strong support for the Confederate cause. Those who had elected to remain with the Union were being harassed, and shooting incidents became a regular occurrence. The following letter from Davidson to the adjutant general, reflects the situation then prevailing.

Headquarters, Camp Fitzgerald, Cal.

Major D. C. Buell   August 10, 1861

Asst. Adjutant-General, Department of the Pacific

Major: I have the honor to enclose the within communications just put in my hands by Major Carleton. I have proposed to the prominent Union men here (General Drown, Abel Stearns, and others) the formation of a home guard for the Town and County of Los Angeles. They responded to the suggestion promptly, and I have promised as soon as they have 100 names enrolled to write to the General and ask for as many stand of arms and ammunition as there are sound Union men. I think the move will have a beneficial effect. I would to God the Union men would hold up their heads more here. I beg the general to believe that with regard to the inclosed subject I will be wary and circumspect, and if prompt action is required on overt acts I will be as quick as the occasion. As the Camp is three-quarters of a mile from where the Depot is, I have ordered an officer and twenty five men to guard the latter nightly, particularly from fire. Should one or two companies be required to lend aid to those companies probably to be sent to San Bernardino, the home guard could be relied upon to take their places in event of difficulty. I am, sir, your obedient servant   JNO. W. DAVIDSON

Captain, First Dragoons, Commanding

One of the letters, enclosed with Davidson's report, written by Matthew Keller to General E. V. Sumner,

THE FOUR DAVIDSON BROTHERS
Standing, left to right: Charles and Roger
Seated, left to right: John W. and Hunter
From a photograph taken at Annapolis, Maryland, January 21, 1870

commanding the Department of the Pacific, dated August 10, 1861, is quoted below, as being highly significant. General Sumner, incidentally, was the one who replaced General Albert Sidney Johnston as the departmental commander.

Sir: I feel it my duty as an old resident of this place to apprise you that all of us who are loyal and devoted to the Stars and Stripes, and that have something to lose in this section of the country, feel that we are in the greatest insecurity as to the public interest as well as to our own lives and property. No part of your command is composed of such discordant and menacing elements as it. Within we have open and avowed secessionists and Southern sympathizers, and I am sorry to say that they are chiefly composed of those who exercise most political influence with the native population, and already they have not failed to poison their minds against the Puritan fanatics of the North. We are threatened with rebellion across the plains by people of the Van Dorn stripe, if we are to credit the repeated efforts of the Texas emigration, and in these disordered times it is well to discredit them. Lower California, the asylum of cut throats and robbers is on our immediate border. We are surrounded to a great extent by barbarous and hostile Indian tribes, that may at any moment be excited against us and the Government by rebels or marauding Mormons. I not only consider it necessary, but to be the part of prudence and timely vigilance, to station a lookout cavalry force at the Cajun Pass, or at some point close thereto. Please to receive my suggestions with indulgence, being made in spirit to subserve public and private interests. Your most obedient servant

MATTHEW KELLER

The second letter, enclosed in Davidson's report, was written by Abel Stearns to General Sumner, dated August 9, 1861. It reiterated the alarm expressed in Mr. Keller's letter, and strongly suggested the assignment of additional troops to Camp Fitzgerald. He also mentioned his regret that Major Carleton and Captain Hancock were assigned to duties elsewhere, then stated,

Those two officers activity and energy have inspired the confidence of the community. In their absence I believe the command to fall upon Captain Davidson, whose long acquaintance with this country and the people I trust may be the means of retaining him amongst us in this position, apart from feelings of friendship for him based upon years of acquaintance.

Davidson lost no time in analyzing the over-all situation, and developing plans for pacifying the area. He then transmitted a plan of action to the adjutant general, Department of the Pacific, in the following communication:

Headquarters, Camp Fitzgerald, Cal.

August 13, 1861

Major D. C. Buell, Asst. Adjutant-General, U.S. Army

Major: After careful thought I have determined, as an officer entrusted with an important command here, to give my views with regard to the dispositions to be made to preserve good order and obedience to the laws in this section of the country. With due deference to older and wiser heads than mine, I believe the arrangement proposed would crush the egg of treason already laid in the Counties of San Bernardino and Los Angeles, give the really good time to listen to the promptings of that patriotism which, however it may be swayed by the passions of the hour, is yet deeply planted in every American heart. Therefore,

1. The depot of supplies for the troops to be at San Pedro, near the mouth of the San Gabriel River; a company of infantry stationed there with temporary work thrown up, and two pieces, or more of Artillery.

2. Two companies of infantry at Los Angeles, either in the town, or at least six miles from it. One months subsistence always on hand.

3. Four companies, two of dragoons and two of infantry, at San Bernardino. I believe if any trouble it will begin there, because of the character of the surrounding population, and the fact that the outlets toward Utah by the Mojave, and toward Texas by the Colorado, invite and tempt by their facilities for escape. By all means keep this squadron of dragoons intact at one point. It is the only body of cavalry in the country and,

with the drill Carleton has given it, is really efficient and can be relied upon for 100 men in the saddle at need. An outpost from the San Bernardino command to be at Martin's ranch, in the Cajon Pass, to consist of an officer and, say, twelve men. Another at Temecula, on the route to Warner's ranch, same number. Both posts to report constantly to San Bernardino. The officer at San Bernardino to have district powers over Los Angeles troops, but not to touch San Pedro. A section of field pieces at Los Angeles and one at San Bernardino. An enterprising officer ought to be able to control at least open acts with these facilities placed at his command. If this arrangement cannot be made, then I respectfully ask authority to move this Camp to San Pedro, and in the advantages of this step all my officers concur with me.

The men are being demoralized here, and I suspect they are being tampered with. The vitality they expend in debauch would be spent in fishing, hunting, boating, and manly exercises. From this point we could mainly control this section of the country. There is a brass field piece here in town (six pounder) belonging, I am told, to the State, now in the hands of the sheriff, Thomas Sanchez, a noted secessionist, which ought, I think, to be in my keeping. Can I get the order of the Governor to deliver it to me, through the general? The home guard about whom I wrote to the general of the date of August 10 have enrolled 100 members, under the accompanying pledge, and I expect to have 100 more within a few days, when their returns come in. Can I have 150 stand of rifles or muskets sent me from the arsenal for issue to them? I will be responsible myself for their safekeeping, and I think these people would be gratified by this mark of the general's confidence. Besides they really need them. There are no arms worth mentioning in the hands of Union men. The fall election comes off September 5, at which time Dimmick, U.S. district attorney, and others fear an outbreak. It would be well if the San Bernardino command could be in position by then. I am, sir, your most obedient Servant,   JNO. W. DAVIDSON
Captain, First Dragoons, Commanding

If the general will grant my suggestion about the arms it is important they should be here before the election comes off on the 7th of September.   J.W.D.

Due to the rabble rousing elements, the situation in and around Los Angeles grew worse, and the morale of the troops deteriorated. As Davidson had pointed out in his letter of August 13, the debauchery of the soldiers sapped their effectiveness, therefore he moved the entire camp to a position outside the town. Of this he reported as follows,

> The camp is on better ground and nearer to the water, the advantages of having less dust to annoy men and horses, and change of scene . . .   Dispensing with drills now and then and encouraging the men to play football and to bathe at those times has had a good effect. They seem to wear a more cheerful air, and the number of desertions has decreased.[3]

Troubles in the outlying areas, caused by roving bands of secessionists harassing the settlers and small settlements between Los Angeles and San Bernardino, rapidly developed into an intolerable situation. Robbery and other crimes were being committed daily. As a consequence, Davidson took to the field with a squadron of ninety Dragoons, on August 31, and headed for San Bernardino. It was his purpose to round up the large groups of secessionists and bandits who were reported to be raiding the settlements of Union sympathizers in that general vicinity. He scouted the entire area around San Bernardino without success, then moved on to the mountain town of Holcomb where a great many deserters had settled. Fortunately for them, they had information about Davidson's movements, and disappeared into the woods before he arrived. Insofar as the rounding up of deserters and the punishing of trouble-

---

[3] The quoted correspondence on the preceding pages is contained in *War of the Rebellion: A Compilation of Official Records of the Union and Confederate Armies,* series I, vol. 50, chapter LXII.

some secessionists was concerned, the mission could be considered a failure. But, the fact that both deserters and secessionists had been dispersed, and the harrassment of Union sympathizers was permanently stopped, the mission was hailed as a highly successful undertaking.

Upon returning to their base camp the Dragoons learned of a change that had taken place in their designation. On August 3, 1861, that branch of the army was re-designated from Dragoons to Cavalry. Hence the First Dragoons became the First U.S. Cavalry. That announcement caused mixed feelings to emerge, and in some cases there were displays of emotion. The Dragoons were mainly disturbed because they were extremely proud of their heritage as elite troops, who had been trained to be highly effective soldiers both mounted and on foot. Cavalrymen, as they knew them, lacked that versatility because their usual training was designed for mounted combat only. The proud Dragoons, especially those who had experienced hard fighting in the far outposts, visualized a loss in the prestige that they had enjoyed. However, they were good, loyal soldiers who soon reconciled themselves to the change.

The air had just cleared from the designation change when the garrison at Camp Fitzgerald was shaken by another change. On November 14, 1861, Captain Davidson was promoted to the rank of Major, and reassigned to the Second Cavalry. The troops of the camp had grown to regard their captain very highly, and felt that his enforced departure was another low blow. However, since the orders specified that Davidson join his new regiment without delay, the garrisoned troops rallied their spirits and gave him a rousing send-off.

Also, due to the urgency of the orders, there was barely enough time for Davidson to pay his final respects to the many civil officials of the community and, of course, there was no opportunity for farewell parties.

Within two days the entire Davidson family was packed out, and on the way to St. Louis. Upon arrival in that city, they moved into the home of Mrs. Davidson's father, George K. McGunnegle. Major Davidson barely paused, then continued on to Washington, D.C., where the Second Cavalry was assigned to the defense of the National Capitol. His tenure in that activity was cut short when, on February 3, 1862, Davidson was promoted to Brevet Brigadier-General of Volunteers. As a consequence, he was ordered to the command of a brigade of cavalry, which formed a part of the Army of the Potomac under the command of General McClellan.

5

War–Sunstroke–Promotions

General Davidson's newly-formed brigade needed much training in order to be prepared for battle, and the time available was short. Fortunately Davidson pushed them hard. They marched south within a month to join the forces preparing for the Peninsular Campaign. The brigade met the enemy very soon, in the "Action of Lees Mills" on April 5, 1862. Those unseasoned troops acquitted themselves better than had been expected and won their first battle, emerging as proud and battle-hardened veterans. There was little activity for some weeks, then they were locked in another fiercely-fought battle on June 26 in the "Action of Mechanicsville." Once again they won the contest. Another short lull was followed in quick succession by the "Battle of Gaines Mills" on June 27, the "Action of Goldings Farm" on June 28, and the "Battle of Savage Station" on June 29, 1862. The Davidson troopers were the victors in all three engagements.

Davidson was awarded two brevet promotions, to Lieutenant Colonel and Colonel, U.S. Army,[1] respec-

---

[1] Brevet (temporary) promotions were freely awarded in the Volunteers, but infrequently in the U.S. Army. The latter were highly prized by career officers for their prestige value, and possible effect upon their future promotions. All career officers expected to revert to their permanent, lower, ranks in the post-war army, but, hopefully, a brevet might hold them at a higher level. Then, too, in later years brevet ranks could be used in official correspondence, for example – a captain may sign an official letter, John Doe, Captain, Brevet Colonel, U.S.A.

tively, for the "Battle of Gaines Mills" and the "Action of Goldings Farm." The weather during those engagements was exceedingly hot and humid, causing much suffering among the troops. In mid-afternoon, during the Battle of Savage Station, Davidson suffered a severe sunstroke. He fell from his horse and had to be carried to the shade of a tree by his orderly, Private William Sharpenburg. At the time it was thought by those present that he was dead. Several years later Captain R. G. Mason, 2nd U.S. Infantry, wrote in a letter,[2]

> I had the honor of serving in General Davidson's Brigade during the summer of 1862, as Colonel of the 7th Regiment. I was with him in the field of Savage Station on June 29 of that year. I saw the General frequently on the march and after we arrived on the field – I think it was about 1 P.M. when the Brigade halted and formed a line of battle in the open field on the left of the railroad. The day was still and intensely hot – the troops were much exhausted with the very long and rapid march, and during the afternoon many officers and men fell in the ranks from the sun. I saw the General frequently after we formed the line – he seemed to feel the severe heat and looked unwell. It was about 3 o'clock when I was informed the General had been – it was feared fatally sunstruck. I had been sick with fever and diarreoa and was hardly able to sit my horse. Soon after we moved into the woods, when I saw the General on the ground looking like a dead man – indeed it was reported that he had died. Sometime afterwards he was placed in an ambulance and removed from the field. Afterwards, while we were in camp in the line General Davidson, more than once, expressed his fear that he had been permanently injured by the sunstroke.

In spite of his brush with death Davidson returned to the action on the following day, much weakened by the effects of the sunstroke. Certainly he was badly needed for, on June 30, another fiercely fought engagement

---

[2] Dated March 17, 1870; in Davidson ACP file.

occurred in the "Battle of Glendale." Upon the conclusion of that battle the entire division, which was
commanded by Major General W. F. Smith, marched
to Ruffin's Farm where they arrived on July 3, 1862,
and went into camp. Under the date of July 11, 1862,
General Smith reported the activities of his division
during the series of battles just ended. In that report,
copy to General Davidson,[3] he commented on the Battle
of Savage Station by saying, "General Davidson had
unfortunately been placed hors-de-combat by a sunstroke while forming his line on the plain." Then his
remarks about the June 30 Battle of Glendale were,

> To General Davidson, overtasked as he had been, was assigned
> the delicate and responsible position of holding the ground until
> the rest of the Division had crossed the two narrow bridges over
> Turkey Creek, of retiring his own Brigade, and then destroying
> the bridges. The duty was performed with perfect success. . .
> [and he concluded with this paragraph:]
>   That the cheerfulness with which the men and officers endured
> the fatigues and privations of this terrible march is above all
> praise. Generals Hancock, Brooks and Davidson deserve, for
> their gallantry and untiring zeal, the especial notice of the Gov-
> ernment.

Responding to the recommendation of the brigade
surgeon, Davidson left for St. Louis on July 24, 1862,
on a thirty-day sick leave to regain his health. While at
home he received orders to take command of the St.
Louis District of the Army of Missouri, on August 7,
1862. This turned out to be a very sensitive position because of the political climate at that time in Missouri.
It was a border state in which a slim majority of the
legislature was pro-Union. The city of St. Louis also

---

[3] In Davidson ACP file.

had sharp divisions, except that the large German-American section of the population was pro-Union. However, there were enough Confederate sympathizers to cause constant trouble, and they harrassed the Union soldiers. This, then, required a strong hand on the part of the military commander to prevent uniformed personnel from retaliating in a violent manner. General Davidson, of course, provided that type of leadership, and thus endeared himself to most of the city's residents.

In southern Missouri and northern Arkansas the tempo of rebel activities increased rapidly in late 1862. General Davidson was directed to command a newly forming Army of Southeast Missouri, to offset that menace. This army also had the ultimate objective of moving against Little Rock, the capital of Arkansas, which was a rebel stronghold. Prior to that it was necessary to drive Confederate General Marmaduke out of Missouri. Marmaduke commanded a brigade of expert horsemen who were terrorizing settlements along the Mississippi River, and in southern Missouri and Arkansas, by guerrilla type raids. At times they would get uncomfortably close to St. Louis. On February 4, 1863, Davidson engaged Marmaduke in battle, and mauled him so badly that the rebel beat a hasty retreat to southern Arkansas to re-group his forces. A few weeks later Marmaduke set out on another raiding expedition in Missouri. Upon learning of this Davidson immediately marched to intercept the rebels. He ran into large pockets of them at Fredericktown, Pilot Knob and Cape Girardeau, and forced them into another hasty retreat. That put brakes on Marmaduke's Missouri activities.

On June 6, 1863, Davidson received orders to take command of a full division of cavalry, then being assembled for the planned assault on Little Rock. Shortly thereafter he was apprised of General Schofield's [4] intentions regarding that operation when he received a copy of that general's telegram [5] to President Lincoln, dated June 5, 1863, in which he said,

> I respectfully recommend Brigadier General J. W. Davidson for promotion to Brevet Major General. He will command the main force in the field of this Department.

Governor Gamble of Missouri added this endorsement, "I concur in this recommendation." There seems to be no doubt that Schofield had nominated Davidson for command of the Little Rock operation that was being organized.

Davidson began assembling his division in the vicinity of Iron Mountain. When his force approached full strength he moved in the direction of Helena, Arkansas, with full intentions of continuing to march in the direction of Little Rock. En route he was advised to use Helena as the staging area. Of Davidson's march the *Chicago Times* published the following news items,

> (Edition of August 4, 1863)   General Davidson's Cavalry Expedition, which left Iron Mountain several weeks ago, has reached Helena, capturing about 500 secession Guerrillas on the way. The original destination of the expedition was Little Rock but, for reasons unknown, it was changed to Helena.

> (Edition of August 11, 1863)   General Steele [6] now outfitting for Little Rock. Gen. Steele came here from Gen. Grant's Army at Vicksburg with specific orders for this purpose. A quarrel developed with General B. N. Prentiss over who was to be the ranking officer. General Hurlbut [7] then ordered General Prentiss to duty elsewhere.

---

[4] Major General J. M. Schofield, Commander, Department of the Missouri.
[5] In Davidson ACP file.   [6] Major General Frederick Steele.
[7] Hurlbut was the corps commander with headquarters in Cairo, Illinois.

(Edition of August 27, 1863) General Steele with the remainder of his forces reached this place (Clarendon) yesterday.
Here they are joined by the splendid Cavalry Division of Brigadier-General Davidson, which recently executed a brilliant
march from Pilot Knob, Missouri, four hundred miles distant.

The record does not indicate just when General
Davidson learned of the orders of General Grant for
General Steele to command the Little Rock expedition.
Certainly it was a bitter pill for him to swallow, since
he believed that honor was justly due him. And it is
not, even now, completely clear as to the extent of
Grant's authority over the Little Rock operation, at
that time. The exchange of correspondence between
Grant, Hurlbut, Schofield, Steele and Davidson indicates that Grant had been asked to send a Division of
Infantry from Vicksburg to operate in the rear of Confederate General Sterling Price, then in Little Rock.
The original intention, apparently, being to prevent
Price from withdrawing to the south while Davidson
made the main assault on Little Rock from the north.
Steele moved his force to Helena to prepare for his
next move. At that time Steele's immediate superior in
the chain of command was General Hurlbut. Schofield
directed Davidson to meet with Steele, at Helena, for
the purpose of arranging a cooperative operation. Then,
on August 1, 1863, Schofield directed Davidson to report to Steele on a temporary basis, but to continue
forwarding his official reports to General Schofield.
That relationship continued throughout the assault on,
and the occupation of Little Rock.[8]

As mentioned earlier, Davidson had, until August 1,

---

[8] The author's interpretation of the correspondence contained in *War of the
Rebellion . . . Official Records, op. cit.*

been confident that he would command the Little Rock expedition. A letter from his father-in-law, George K. McGunnegle, dated August 24, confirms this by saying to Davidson,[9]

> You seem still impressed with the opinion that Gen. Steele was given the command at the insistence of Gen. Schofield – if such be the fact then the latter has been guilty of the utmost duplicity, for he assured us most earnestly that he regretted General Grant's having interfered in his plans by placing Steele there – Seeing that Steele had reached Helena to take command I made it my business to see the Generals and mention what the papers said about Steele taking the command which induced the remark made by Schofield, all of which I wrote you immediately on my return to the office, stating that I thought the Generals very friendly disposed towards you.

Although terribly disappointed at the turn of events, there is no indication that Davidson permitted it to have an adverse effect upon his performance during the Little Rock campaign. When he joined Steele at Clarendon, Arkansas, on August 17, 1863, the two engaged in a lengthy conference to develop their plans for the forthcoming assault, and finally decided to employ a pincers movement. About that time an intelligence report reached Steele indicating that Davidson's West Point classmate, Confederate General Kirby Smith, was rapidly nearing Little Rock with a large force to relieve the pressure on the city. Davidson expressed his belief that they could cope with the situation, but Steele became very concerned about their ability to handle that menace. Probably that feeling on Steele's part was induced by the serious weakening of his force by sickness. He expressed his concern in a letter to General

---

[9] Original letter in the author's file.

Hurlbut, dated August 23, saying, "If you do not send reinforcements, I shall very likely meet with disaster." [10] Some time later it was found that General Smith actually was in Shreveport, with no intention of moving to Little Rock.

When their plans were finalized Davidson moved toward Little Rock on the south side of the Arkansas River. Steele followed later along the north side of the river. At Brownsville (now Lonoke, Arkansas) Davidson ran into Marmaduke's cavalry, and a short skirmish ensued. The rebels were dislodged and driven about nine miles to the west, leaving Confederate General Walker, a brigade commander, in Davidson's hands. That general was thoroughly pumped for information, but he refused to cooperate. Marmaduke took up a position at Bayou Meto, in accordance with previously issued instructions to hold that point for as long as possible. Davidson, however, allowed no time for the enemy to dig in, and attacked at noon on August 27. When Confederate General Sterling Price, in Little Rock, received Marmaduke's report of the attack, he reported to his superiors that the attack was "with greatly superior numbers, and considerable spirit." [11]

In truth, Davidson had considered the ground to be unfavorable for committing his entire force, and only attacked with one dismounted brigade and a battalion of infantry. It will be remembered that Davidson's troopers were trained as dragoons, and fully capable of fighting effectively on foot or in the saddle. That force pushed the rebels from two of their positions, and back to a strongly entrenched camp about a mile east of the

---

[10] Kenneth P. Williams, *Lincoln Finds a General, vol. 5: Prelude to Chattanooga.*   [11] *Ibid.*

Bayou. The First Iowa Cavalry then boldly dashed in, through a heavy fire, and drove Marmaduke's forces back across the river. That action was the key one that cleared the way for the main assault on Little Rock.

The next few days were spent in making final preparations for the big push. During this time another intelligence report alarmed Steele still further, and he reported to Schofield,[12]

> The enemy has collected just about everything he has in front of Little Rock. – General Kirby Smith, a highly capable commander, was sending in everything he can gather from his Department of the Trans-Mississippi. Smith had been heard to say that if he could not hold Little Rock he could not hold Texas.

The rebel defenders took up a position three miles north of the city in a heavily wooded swamp, with about 14,000 men. Steele's and Davidson's combined troop strength amounted to less than 12,000 men. Knowing this, Schofield sent an urgent dispatch to the General-in-Chief of the Army, General Halleck, outlining the situation and asking for reinforcements. In turn Halleck directed that surplus troops from the Department of the Northwest be sent to assist Steele. However, Steele and Davidson agreed that any further delay might jeopardize the entire operation, and decided to attack immediately. Steele set out on September 6 for the Arkansas River, while Davidson and his cavalry cleared the route ahead. Considering the information available at the time, that was an exceptionally bold move, unsurpassed for its timing and ultimate results. It is especially true when one realizes that the forces of Steele and Davidson were moving against superior numbers of men who were thoroughly familiar with the area, while

---

[12] *Ibid.*

the bluecoats knew nothing of the ground to be covered.

On September 10 Davidson crossed the Arkansas River in order to approach Little Rock on the south side of the city. A short time later, at Bayou Fourche, he ran into heavy opposition from Marmaduke's forces who were waiting in ambush. The *New York Times,* edition of September 27, 1863, describes the ensuing action in these terms,

> While crossing the Arkansas River at Bayou Fourche the rebel fire was extremely heavy from 3 sides, and Davidson's advance company came tumbling back over the batteries, followed by the rebels, who swarmed from their hiding places, and, with a savage cry, made a grand rush for the guns.
>
> Completely disordered by the suddenness of the attack, and what they conceived to be the loss of their Colonel, the regiment fell back with great precipitancy until checked by General Davidson, who dashed among them and rallied them once more into line, while under the enemy's fire. They rallied and drove the rebels, pell mell, back across the open space.

General Steele, on the opposite side of the river, saw great clouds of smoke and dust rising on Davidson's side, and feared the movement of a strong force of rebels against Davidson. He, therefore, sent a dispatch instructing Davidson to withdraw to a safer position near the river. Instead, Davidson had other ideas and continued advancing to the outskirts of the city, then mounted a brisk charge. While galloping to the city Davidson learned that, instead of advancing, General Price was in full retreat. Later Price made the statement that, "I am not going to get caught in a trap like some of the other commanders had done." [13]

At seven o'clock in the evening Davidson led his

_____
[13] *Ibid.*

troops into Little Rock, and accepted its surrender from the acting civil authorities. Early in the morning of the next day General Steele marched into the city. They found that General Price had been in such a rush to get out of Little Rock that he had not destroyed valuable supplies and materials, including the arsenal.

When General Steele arrived in the city he immediately designated General Davidson to be the military governor, by issuing his General Order #22, dated Sept. 10, 1863.

It is well worth noting the conduct of the cavalrymen when they rode into the city, which is well covered as follows,[14]

General Orders #62   Cavalry Division of Missouri
                                        Little Rock, Sept. 13, 1863
Soldiers of the Cavalry Division I congratulate you on your victory, capture of Little Rock. You have gained two victories on the same day. Flushed with success you entered the city in darkness when you could not be seen – your passions stirred by seeing comrades fall – yet no outrages upon the defenseless inhabitants has stained your hands.

I thank you from the bottom of my heart.

                                        J. W. DAVIDSON

General Steele made a detailed report of the operation on September 12, 1863, enclosing Davidson's report, and forwarded it to General Schofield. In it he made several references to the excellence of Davidson's generalship, and concluded with,

The operations of this Army, from the time that I commenced organizing it at Helena, has occupied exactly forty days. Our entire loss in killed, wounded and prisoners will not exceed 100. The enemy's is much greater, especially in prisoners, at least

_____
[14] *War of the Rebellion . . . Official Records, op. cit.,* series I, vol. 22, parts 1 and 2.

1000. I shall reserve the list of casualties and my special recommendations for a future communication. However, I will say that Davidson and his Cavalry Division deserve the highest commendation.

There was, however, another letter that probably gave Davidson a greater feeling of pride than any other. It is,[15]

General J. W. Davidson   September 16, 1963
Dear Sir: Permit me, though in humble position, to congratulate you upon the felicity of your plan of attack and movement of your troops and your complete success in capturing Little Rock. It is a consumation which will gladden thousands of loyal hearts. It was my good fortune to witness your bravery and skill in the movement of your forces. During life I shall hold you in admiration. May you support *another* star.
                                           JOHN M. COGGLESHELL
                                  Chaplain 1st Iowa Cavalry Vols.

Additional honors were contained in the following excerpt from a news item published in the September 16, 1863, edition of the *Chicago Times,*

The operations of Gen. Davidson's cavalry have been daring in the extreme. Their rapid movements, and the bold manner in which they have pressed upon the enemy, have led the rebels to suppose that Gen. Steele's whole army was upon them.   .   .

Davidson's cavalry division is undoubtedly the finest body of cavalry on the continent, and each member is sanguine of its ability to accomplish anything within the range of possibilities. The rebels have a most prudent dread of its approach, and make no secret of it. Neither day or night passes without signaling some daring act, conceived and executed by it.

The *St. Louis Union,* edition of September 22, 1863, published a lengthy account of the operation, and concluded with,

---
[15] Davidson ACP file.

The whole country owes to General Davidson, and the army under his command, a debt of gratitude. A more valuable service has not been rendered by any officer.

A most gratifying tribute to his generalship was contained in a letter written by General Schofield to General Halleck, dated November 3, 1863.[16] It says,

I would consider myself as doing less than justice to a meritorious officer, and to the country, did I not add an especial recommendation in Gen'l. Davidson's case. On my assignment to this command I organized a Cavalry Division for operation against the rebels in Arkansas. It was made up of regiments which had been serving in various parts of Missouri, and attached to different brigades of the Frontier, entirely unaccustomed to the operations of Cavalry in large bodies. By constant and untiring labor, and strict discipline, Gen'l. Davidson has brought this body of men into the finest condition of any body of cavalry in the United States. Certainly it will challenge comparison with any other. My success, heretofore, has been due to no officer more than to Gen'l. Davidson, and I hope that the Government may be pleased to give him that promotion, which I believe he has so justly merited.

The final weeks of 1863 turned into a period of frustration and aggravation for General Davidson. He had suffered a severe blow to his pride during the second half of the year, when he lost the command that had been promised. Throughout the entire year letters by the dozen from prominent individuals, recommendations from the governors of several states, and petitions from state legislatures, had been sent to the President, and others, urging his promotion to major general. But all were to no avail. On top of those irritations a new one arose. As military governor of Little Rock he established policies covering the status and treatment of city

---

16 Copy in Davidson ACP file.

residents. They included a policy of firmness in dealing with those who had supported the rebels, and had refused to take an oath of allegiance to the Union. And Davidson demanded strict enforcement of those policies. General Steele, on the other hand, seemed to favor a policy of ultra-leniency. He began to interfere with Davidson's conduct of his responsibilities, something the latter resented.

There is ample evidence that some "feeling" had existed between Davidson and Steele from the beginning of their association. It is certain that Davidson envied Steele in his position as the commander of the Little Rock expedition, since it was an assignment he felt was justly his. Then, all during the campaign, it appeared that Davidson received the lion's share of praise for the conduct of an operation commanded by Steele, causing Steele to feel slighted. Probably these suppressed feelings surfaced when the two sat down to discuss their differences over the treatment to be accorded the citizens of Little Rock. In such an atmosphere the language could easily become over-heated, and cause the passing of an insult or two. According to the *Arkansas Gazette* historical review of the entire situation, published in twelve installments during late 1963 and early 1964, Steele called Davidson a "radical." At that time it was considered, by many, to be a most unsavory term. It infuriated Davidson.

The quarrel raged for several days, then a private letter, written by Davidson to a friend about the situation, was published in the *Missouri Democrat,* edition of January 5, 1864. It was done without Davidson's knowledge or consent. That infuriated Steele, and it was feared by many that the two would fight a duel.

Fortunately that was averted. But Steele then arranged with General Halleck to have Davidson relieved of his command. Brigadier General E. A. Carr was ordered as a replacement, and the change in command occurred on January 31, 1864. Davidson proceeded to Cairo, Illinois, to await reassignment. While there he complained bitterly to his superiors, and directly to President Lincoln about the unfairness involved in the loss of a command he cherished.[17] There is no indication that any of those appeals bore fruit. However, according to the *Arkansas Gazette* edition of February 9, 1964, Senator Wade, chairman of the Senate Committee on the Conduct of the War, upon hearing of Steele's action, requested Davidson to furnish a detailed report of the entire situation. He also asked for Davidson's evaluation of "the manner in which Steele administered the affairs of his command." Davidson complied and, as stated in the *Gazette,* "His [Davidson's] appraisal of Steele's military administration was to cost Steele his command."

On March 11, 1864, General Davidson was ordered to return to St. Louis and take command of the West Division Cavalry Bureau. The most difficult task, while in this position, was to procure 30,000 cavalry horses for Major General E. R. S. Canby, Commander, Military Division of West Mississippi, with headquarters in New Orleans. It was a monumental task because the region, for miles around, had been thoroughly scoured for suitable cavalry mounts. However, Davidson dispatched scouts to all parts of Missouri and neighboring states, and the orders were soon filled.

---

[17] *War of the Rebellion* . . . *Official Records, op. cit.,* series I, vol. 34, part 2.

While in St. Louis, on May 12, 1864, Davidson was the recipient of one of the highest honors that could be conferred upon an officer. He was visited in his office by a committee from the 1st Iowa Cavalry, composed of one sergeant from each of the eleven companies, and one sergeant from the headquarters staff. They presented him with a ceremonial sword made of the best possible material, enclosed in a scabbard of gold and silver overlaid with gold. The handle is beautifully made and richly studded with diamonds, and the whole is carried in a neat case for preservation when not in use. Accompanying the sword was the following letter, dated May 12, 1864,[18]

> General J. W. Davidson: In the name of the non-commissioned officers and privates of the 1st Iowa Cavalry, I have the honor to present you this sabre as a testimonial of your gallant conduct as an officer devoted to the interests of your country and your men – as a brave and self-sacrificing soldier, and as a loyal true hearted man. We know it will ever be drawn in the defense of the liberty and honor of our glorious country. General, I am a soldier, and believing in actions rather than words, I will only add that the 1st Iowa Veteran Cavalry desires no other honor than to be led by the hero of Bayou Metre, and Little Rock.
>
> H. L. MORRILL, Sergeant

The General responded with many warm and appropriate remarks, and formalized the presentation with this letter, dated May 12, 1864,[19]

> Sergeant H. L. Morrill and command of 1st Iowa Cavalry:
> I accept the sword which you give as a trust to be kept in my family, an incentive in all future time to make myself worthy of those who bestow it. In honoring me you honor yourselves, for whatever I enjoy, whatever of service I may have been to our

---

[18] Copy in Davidson ACP file, National Archives; and in Smithsonian Institution.   [19] Copy in Davidson ACP file.

beloved country, is due in great part to your manly support and the valor of your arms.

I accept further as a symbol — a symbol of that brotherhood which unites us from the rocking pines of New England to the sunny prairies of the West, under the folds of a common flag to do battle in the cause of Union and human liberty.

Henceforward then, whenever my hand grasps the hilt, I will feel that I am grasping the hand of each member of your noble regiment, and that a thousand of you are watching my actions.

And, in after life when our armed heels have crushed the head of this serpent, treason — should sickness or misfortune befall one of your number it will be a sure passport to my home for him to say, "I was of the 1st Iowa Cavalry."   J. W. DAVIDSON

That sword is now on permanent loan to the Smithsonian Institution for display in the military section. It is, incidentally, one of the very few ever given a commander by the enlisted men.

In June 1864, Davidson was ordered to New Orleans as Chief of the Cavalry Bureau, Military Division of West Mississippi. In that capacity he reported directly to General Canby, the commander of the division, whose jurisdiction included the Department of Arkansas, commanded by General Steele. General Davidson's area of jurisdiction extended over some twenty regiments of cavalry that were scattered among the various departments in the division. A review of the correspondence during that period indicates that Steele became very concerned because of Davidson's influential position with General Canby. However, there is no indication that Davidson exerted any adverse influence. En route to his post in New Orleans, Davidson made a momentary stop in Baton Rouge where a large body of cavalry was being assembled. He gained the impression that these troops were below an acceptable standard, and requested the Assistant Inspector-General of the Di-

vision to make a detailed inspection of the situation.
Major J. E. Cowan, the incumbent of that office, complied and submitted his report on August 11, 1864. He
stated that the troops were poorly trained, their horses
ill-fed, and that discipline was very lax. Davidson endorsed the report to General Canby, who took prompt
action by removing and replacing most of the higher
ranking officers.

General Canby directed Davidson, on November 11,
1864, to organize and command an expedition to march
from Baton Rouge to Pascagoula, Mississippi. The
orders read, in part,[20]

> Operate from Baton Rouge, Louisiana, to divert the enemy cav-
> alry from General Sherman's right flank, and to cut the Mobile
> & Ohio Railroad south of Meridian.

Davidson proceeded to Baton Rouge, and began assembling the force he would lead. It had been planned
to consist of one full division of cavalry, plus two bat-
teries of horse artillery to a total in excess of 3,000
troops. Since time was of the essence a night and day
drill schedule was put into effect for the purpose of
welding troop units, from widely separated areas, into
an effective, hard-hitting expeditionary force. Davidson
drove himself as hard as the men, and they soon responded to the man they acknowledged to be a master of
his profession.

The expedition moved out of Baton Rouge on November 27, 1864. That date just happened to be one
year after General Grant, under the date of November
27, 1863, wrote to General Halleck recommending that
such an expedition be made at the earliest possible date.

---

[20] *Army and Navy Journal,* Jan. 7, 1865.

The Ceremonial Sword and its Hilt
Presented to Davidson by
men of the First Iowa Cavalry
at St. Louis, May 12, 1864.
Engraving on the blade reads
"bayou metre – US – little rock"

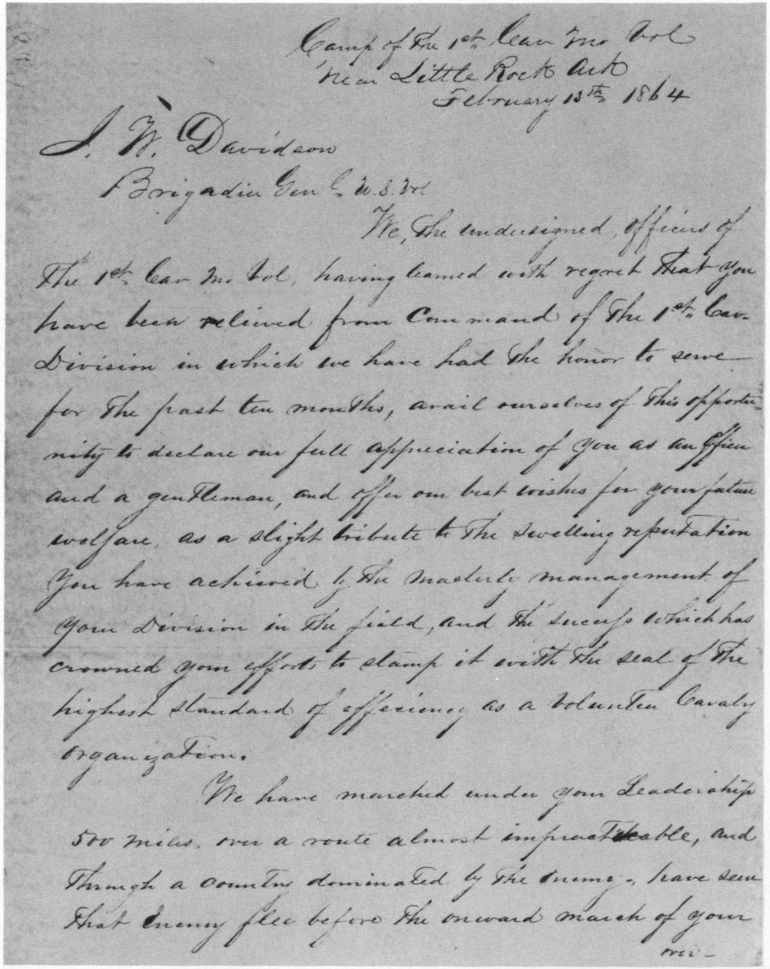

Camp of the 1st Cav Mo Vol
near Little Rock Ark
February 13th 1864

J. W. Davidson
Brigadier Genl U.S. Vol

We, the undersigned, Officers of the 1st Cav Mo Vol, having learned with regret that you have been relieved from Command of the 1st Cav. Division in which we have had the honor to serve for the past ten months, avail ourselves of this opportunity to declare our full appreciation of you as an Officer and a gentleman, and offer our best wishes for your future welfare, as a slight tribute to the swelling reputation you have achieved by the masterly management of your Division in the field, and the success which has crowned your efforts to stamp it with the seal of the highest standard of efficiency as a Volunteer Cavalry organization.

We have marched under your Leadership 500 miles, over a route almost impracticable, and through a country dominated by the enemy, have seen that enemy flee before the onward march of your

THE APPRECIATION LETTER FROM THE OFFICERS OF THE FIRST CAVALRY MISSOURI VOLUNTEERS

... examine the columns, enlist he was finally
shown from the defence of Fitch Rest — and
the flag which you had held still full with admirer
trans over the Capitol of another State redeemed from
the curse of rebellion!

Respectfully inscribed, as we are, with
your worth as an officer, your certainty and that
tact as a gentleman, and the sympathy we hereafter
for each other as soldiers fighting in defence of the
sacred trust of Liberty and Union — we can not suffer
you to depart without this little expression of our
regard, and the hope that in other field common
duties with your friend ability, may soon invite you
and an opportunity be offered to render it available
as you have the one you are now leaving.

With the assurance of our continued
regard and admiration we remain, General,

Very respectfully, yours the Union,

Major Gen. Fitch. Baxley County,
Capt. Brig. Gen.

Gen. E. Lynch, Surgeon, 1st Mich. Vols.
James P. Cooy, 1st Lt. & Regt. Comy
B. Y. Green, 1st Lt.
Wm. H. Brown, Sergt. Co. C.
A. J. Willis, Capt. Co. C.
Henry Clum, Lieut. Co. C.
W. Hanna, Capt. Co. A. 1st Car. Mich.
Richard Still, Lieut. Co. B.
Geo. Swayer, Capt. Co. D. 1st Vol.
Wm. J. Hews, Lieut. & Capt. 1st Vol. Inf. Inf.
N. Col. M. B. Wyer, Capt. Col. 1st Car. Mer. Va.
Wm. White, 1st Lieut. Co. 1st Car.
J. Grove, 1st Lieut. Co. H.
John D. Ames, 2nd Lieut. Co.
C. H. Hopkins, 1st Lieut. Cartersport
John Bend, Captain Co. B. 1st Car. Mer. Vol.

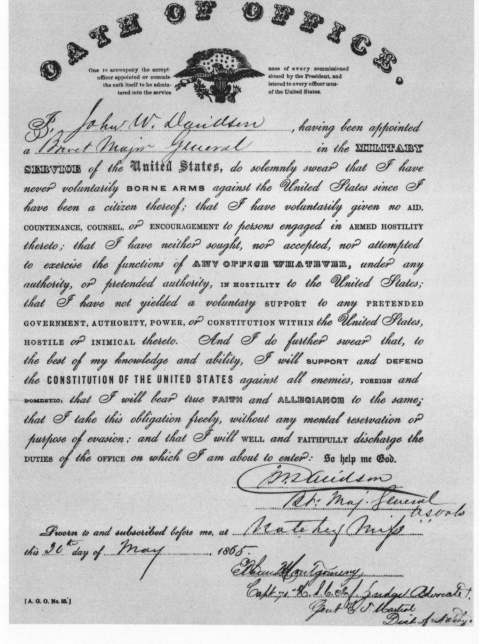

OATH OF OFFICE.

One to accompany the acceptance of every commissioned officer appointed or commissioned by the President, and the oath itself to be administered to every officer mustered into the service of the United States.

I, *John W. Davidson*, having been appointed a *Brevet Major General* in the MILITARY SERVICE of the United States, do solemnly swear that I have never voluntarily BORNE ARMS against the United States since I have been a citizen thereof; that I have voluntarily given no AID, COUNTENANCE, COUNSEL, or ENCOURAGEMENT to persons engaged in ARMED HOSTILITY thereto; that I have neither sought, nor accepted, nor attempted to exercise the functions of ANY OFFICE WHATEVER, under any authority, or pretended authority, IN HOSTILITY to the United States; that I have not yielded a voluntary SUPPORT to any PRETENDED GOVERNMENT, AUTHORITY, POWER, or CONSTITUTION WITHIN the United States, HOSTILE or INIMICAL thereto. And I do further swear that, to the best of my knowledge and ability, I will SUPPORT and DEFEND the CONSTITUTION OF THE UNITED STATES against all enemies, FOREIGN and DOMESTIC; that I will bear true FAITH and ALLEGIANCE to the same; that I take this obligation freely, without any mental reservation or purpose of evasion; and that I will WELL and FAITHFULLY discharge the DUTIES of the OFFICE on which I am about to enter: So help me God.

J M Davidson
Bt. Maj. General
U.S. Vols

Sworn to and subscribed before me, at *Natchez Miss* this 30th day of *May*, 1865.

Wm Montgomery
Capt. 71 N. S. C. Inf. Judge Advocate.
Prvt. & F. Martial
Dist of Natchez.

[A. G. O. No. 55.]

DAVIDSON'S OATH OF OFFICE AS BREVET MAJOR GENERAL
This appointment to this rank in the Volunteers was
as of March 13, 1865, and the oath dated May 30.
On October 3 of 1866 he signed the same oath for his
appointment to the same rank in the United States Army.

In that recommendation Grant suggested that "General Davidson and his splendid division of cavalry be assigned to this operation." [21]

Probably the best possible description of the problems and difficulties of that march can be portrayed in the report submitted by Davidson to Canby, dated December 13, 1864,[22]

> My command is arriving at this point [West Pascagoula, Mississippi]. Our only losses are only 1 officer and 2 men killed, 8 men wounded, and 13 men missing, principally stragglers captured by the enemy. The bad weather and horrible condition of the roads impeded our march so far as to destroy one of the essential elements of success, celerity. We had to lay pontoons four times – over the Amite, Pearl and Black Rivers, and Red Creek; repair and rebuild upwards of fifteen bridges, burned or washed away; and laid miles of corduroy over the swamps of Louisiana and Mississippi, through country so poor as to render the transportation of subsistence a matter of necessity. Our route has been through Greensburg, Franklinton, Fordville, Columbia, Augusta – part of the command over the Leaf and Chickasee Rivers – to this point. The day after my arrival at Augusta, I found Mobile papers, herewith enclosed, containing full accounts of strengths and designs; and our daily marches and progress were telegraphed to Meridian, where General R. Taylor had transferred his headquarters, and to Mobile. . .
>
> On account of the state of the roads and swollen condition of the streams, and their perfect knowledge of our movements, celerity and surprise were impossibilities. To have crossed a wheel over the Pascagoula would not only, in my opinion, have involved the loss of our artillery and pontoons, but most probably without the power of inflicting compensating damage upon the enemy. Weighing well the facts and chances, I decided to move my command to this point, to be transferred to East Pascagoula, from whence a constant series of threats and attacks may be made upon

---

[21] *War of the Rebellion* . . . *Official Records, op. cit.,* series I, vol. 34, part 2. [22] *Ibid.*

the railroad. My decision, when made, was submitted to my
division commanders, Brigadier General Bailey and Colonel E. J.
Davis, and entirely concurred in by them both. Much of the information given me of the country was incorrect. I was informed
that the Pearl and Pascagoula Rivers needed only 200 feet of
bridge to cross them, and that, running between high banks, a
rise in their waters did not materially increase their width. This
is incorrect. When up, they both spread over wide bottoms, and
the Pascagoula, at Holden's was over 600 feet wide. I had carried
100 feet of bridge more than I was advised to do, but was unable
to cross at that place.

The report concluded with the statement that Davidson
would turn the command over to General Bailey, so he
could return to his duties in New Orleans.

Evidently Davidson's decision to avoid moving on to
Mobile, and to the railroad, was a sound one, because
the rebels knew every move he made, and were prepared to offer strong resistance. Rebel troops were
pouring into the area from many different points, in
response to a series of urgent dispatches from the Confederate commander in Mobile, Major General Dab-
ney H. Maury. During the period of December 1 to 4,
1864, that commander had sent out seven dispatches to
other military commanders, and to state governors,
asking for reinforcing troops to repel the approaching
Davidson. One typical dispatch, on December 1, went
to Brigadier General D. W. Adam, saying, "Enemy left
Tangipahoa this morning under Davidson, 4,000 cavalry. Send all the men you have." [23]

As a result of those dispatches Maury had assembled
more than eight thousand troops to greet Davidson if
and when he attempted to cross the river. All of these
additional men were drawn from forces that had been

[23] *Ibid.,* series I, vol. 45, part 2.

committed to the opposition of General Sherman as he marched towards the sea. There seems little doubt that this siphoning off of troops had some beneficial effect upon the outcome of Sherman's march. How much may never be known.

That Davidson created a near panic among the rebels in Mississippi was indicated when Canby reported progress to the General-in-Chief of the Army, General Halleck, on December 4, 1864. Among other things he said, "He [Davidson] has been successful. He had caused quite a panic in Mobile, and was reported as devastating the country generally." [24]

The *Army & Navy Journal,* edition of January 7, 1865, covers the expedition in the following terms,

> General Davidson left Baton Rouge with a force of 4200 in two divisions . . . for an invasion of Mississippi, in cooperation with Sherman's double campaign. On Dec. 1st he reached Tanghipaho, destroyed miles of the Jackson RR and burned the conscript camp, RR bridges and buildings.
>
> Gov. Clarke (Alabama) issued a proclamation for his reserves to come out, and McCulloch's cavalry was rallied to oppose the march. The railroad was destroyed at Franklinville. Scott's cavalry (rebel) now began to oppose us, and on the 2nd a sharp skirmish occurred, on Yazoo City and Vicksburg road. . . Arrived at Pascagoula on the 12th; traveled 280 miles over wretched roads, swamps and forests in 15 days.

During the expedition supplies for the troops and animals ran dangerously low. Forage for animals was extremely meager. Fortunately for the men, the country through which they passed happened to be a rich growing area for sweet potatoes and peanuts. Many was the time when the only subsistence was those sweet potatoes and peanuts. They were very tiresome but

---

24 *Ibid.,* series I, vol. 45, part 1.

nourishing. The soldiers, in the grim humor that is characteristic of fighting men the world over, dubbed the expedition, "The Sweet Potato Raid." [25]

Shortly after his report of December 13, General Davidson left his command in the hands of General Bailey and returned to New Orleans. Upon arrival he was running a high fever, evidently an outgrowth of his exposure during the march through mosquito-infested swamps. A hindsight analysis of the description of that illness indicates that it must have been a severe attack of malaria. He recovered within a few days, in time to receive notification of a new assignment. It was to command the District of Natchez, Department of Mississippi, with headquarters in the city of Natchez. He arrived in Natchez, and assumed the command on January 3, 1865. The quarters assigned for him and family was one of the finest mansions in the city, and was comfortably staffed with servants.

Davidson's first report that he had formally assumed the command was made on January 8. In it he outlined some of the problems to be solved. The military forces of the area were substandard, and the city government left much to be desired. He then outlined the steps he intended taking to correct the deficiencies. The point was made that an adequate level of military preparedness could not be achieved unless one additional regiment was assigned at the earliest possible time. A following letter, to General Canby on January 17, stated,[26]

---

[25] St. Louis Republican, June 29, 1881, quoting William Sharpenburg of the St. Louis police force who had been Davidson's orderly throughout the Civil War.

[26] *War of the Rebellion* . . . *Official Records,* series I, vol. 50.

I consider the necessity to be urgent. It is very important to have officers at the picket-lines of sufficient intelligence to understand the orders issued by the general commanding the military division, upon the application of parties claiming to own or control the products beyond our lines, and upon permission to take out supplies, even after having been duly issued at my headquarters. . . The officers of outposts should certainly have intelligence enough to conduct the preliminary examination, and satisfy himself of the good faith of the parties being brought within the lines.

It seems that the city authorities, of long standing, either could not or would not conform to the policies established by the military commander, and there simply were not enough officers to oversee their operations. One item that was reported to General Canby, on February 4, concerned a General Brayman who had been placed in charge of a Freedmen's Camp and a number of plantations across the river. It was discovered that this general had established, "the most merciless despotism ever heard of, over these people." Davidson also found that,

General Brayman had also taken a pair of very fine horses from a Mrs. John Minor who had taken the oath of allegiance. . . Instead of turning them over for Government use he put them in his private use.[27]

Within a short time most of the troublesome officers were removed and replaced, including General Brayman, and the district problems began to diminish.

The happiest news of many years arrived in Natchez when, on March 13, 1865, Davidson was promoted to Major General of Volunteers. The letter of appointment read, in part, "To Brevet Major General U.S.

---

[27] *Ibid.*

Volunteers for gallant and conspicuous service during the War." [28]

At long last Davidson received the recognition that was justly deserved for the many contributions he made to the war's successful prosecution. Although highly elated he still hoped the same brevet would be awarded in the regular army, and the honor eventually came, but not until mid-1866, to rank from the same date, March 13, 1865.

Although the war was rapidly nearing an end the problems in the Natchez region began to increase once again. This time the causes were from a different source. Large numbers of rebel soldiers, realizing their cause was hopeless, began to desert and attempt to escape across the Mississippi River. The Union forces were charged with the task of preventing this, and much of that preventive effort centered around the Natchez area. Those escape efforts increased after General Lee surrendered to General Grant on April 9, 1865. Then on May 31, Davidson was highly gratified when Lieutenant General J. B. Hood and his staff surrendered to him. It was learned that these Confederate officers had been foiled in an attempt to escape across the river, and were left with no choice but to surrender. General Davidson placed these officers on parole under the terms of General Order No. 61, Military Division of West Mississippi.[29]

Following the assassination of President Lincoln on April 14, 1865, memorial services were held in his honor throughout the country. In Natchez, on April 17, 1865, similar services and a parade were held.

---

[28] Davidson ACP file.
[29] *War of the Rebellion* . . . *Official Records,* series I, vol. 50.

Davidson was the grand marshal of the parade. That is the first and only time General Davidson wore the saber that was presented to him by the 1st Iowa Cavalry.

On June 1, 1865, the scope of Davidson's command was broadened by adding the command of the Southern District of Mississippi. He thereupon decided to make an inspection tour of this new area. On June 22 he set out on that inspection, with a small detachment and the post surgeon, and headed for the southern boundary of the district, some two hundred miles distant. After eighty-five miles were covered Davidson became violently ill. The surgeon advised an immediate return to Natchez. His report dated August 10, 1865, stated,[30]

General Davidson had been overcome, as the weather was exceedingly hot. The attack was as though sunstroke, and it would have been extremely hazardous to his health to proceed any further. I advised an immediate return, and we started back, traveling by easy stages, during the cool part of early morning and evening only. His symptoms were of one who had previously suffered a sunstroke. I hereby declare my opinion and belief that service in southern latitudes would seriously involve the health of General Davidson, if not actually endanger his life.

In response to the surgeon's recommendation Davidson took a leave of absence, in order to recuperate. On January 17, 1866, he was offered a new assignment, to command the Second Cavalry Regiment, at Fort Riley, Kansas. That seemed to be an indication of his post-war status, since the command of a cavalry regiment warranted the rank of colonel. Naturally he accepted with alacrity.

---

[30] Davidson ACP file.

6

Seventh and Tenth Cavalry

At the end of a short leave of absence Davidson reported, on March 6, 1866, for the new assignment as Commander, Second Cavalry, at Fort Riley, Kansas. This was at the time when the army was entering the final phase of reducing the war-time strength, of more than one million men, to the authorized peace time total of 54,000 officers and men. Most of the career officers dropped back to their permanent ranks, and therefore Davidson reverted to Major. However, he was immediately breveted to Colonel in order to retain command of his regiment. The process of determining the officers to be retained, and their ranks in the post-war army, was about to begin. That, of course, became a painful task for those who were to make these selections, because an excessive number of both regular and volunteer officers clamored for retention at, or near to, their highest brevet. Inevitably many inequities were bound to occur, some because of favoritism, quite a large number due to political influence, and others as a result of misguided selections.

The task of making final selections was assigned to a specially organized Selection Board, with Major General William T. Sherman as its president. In an effort to insure fairness to all concerned the Assistant Adjutant General of the Army, Major General E. D. Townsend, directed all commanders to submit data on those sub-

ordinates who should be considered by the board. Upon
receipt of that directive Davidson forwarded the information on the officers of the regiment, then wrote the
following letter to General Townsend, dated March 10,
1866,[1]

> General: I have just seen Special Order No. 92, of the Lieu-
> tenant General, and have the honor, under it, to forward copies
> of certain special letters of my commanders, to be laid before the
> Board of which Major General Sherman is President, in addition
> to the official Reports on file in your office. I do this in justice to
> myself because I have not been fortunate enough to serve con-
> tinuously with one army throughout the War, and my record is
> scattered through the history of the Army of the Potomac, the
> Military Division of the West Mississippi, the Department of
> Missouri, the Department of Kansas, the Department of Mis-
> sissippi, and the West Division of the Cavalry Bureau. I presume
> the originals of most of these letters thus forwarded are, however,
> or have been sent to your office.

With the foregoing letter off his mind Davidson
turned full attention to the multitude of difficult problems needing solutions before an efficient and effective
regiment could be developed. It was, incidentally, necessary to create a fighting regiment out of the flood of
raw recruits that were pouring in. To assist him were a
pitifully small number of experienced non-coms and
junior officers, and practically no seasoned troops. In
the beginning, therefore, Davidson bore the brunt of
the burden, since he was the only one with a strong
enough background of experience to do the job. Consequently he gave no further thought to his ultimate
status. By the first of June the regimental "shaping-up"
had progressed to a point where its commander could
be spared for other temporary duties. The department

---

[1] Davidson ACP file.

commander, therefore, sent Davidson off on an inspection tour of the Department of Missouri. While on that assignment Davidson's hopes for a permanent commission as colonel were given a boost when, in July 1866, Congress authorized four new cavalry regiments to be added to the post-war army. They were designated the 7th through the 10th, with the 7th to be formed at Fort Riley. Certainly one in Davidson's position would naturally expect to become the permanent commander of one of the new regiments, or to retain the one he held temporarily.

His expectations for the future seemed brighter than ever when, upon returning from the inspection tour, Davidson received the following directive from the Departmental Commander, dated August 27, 1866,[2]

Special Orders No. 2. Bvt. Maj. General John W. Davidson, Major 2nd U.S. Cavalry is hereby detailed to take charge of and superintend the organization of the new Regiment of Cavalry at Fort Riley, Kansas. He will select from the subalterns of the 2nd U.S. Cavalry a suitable number of officers to assist in the organization, but not to take such a number as to interfere with the efficiency of the Regiment. Not more than one of every seventy-five recruits should be detailed on this duty until the Regimental organization is announced from Washington, and at least one officer per company arrives to replace those retained.

By Command of Major General Hancock
/s/ Assistant Adjutant General

Davidson began organizing the 7th Cavalry Regiment on September 10, 1866, and immediately embarked upon a rigorous training program. There is little doubt that he fully expected to be designated the regimental commander, with the rank of colonel. He gave generously of his time, experience and energy in

---

[2] *Ibid.*

an effort to create one of the finest cavalry regiments in
the army. Due to his enthusiasm the organization and
training proceeded at a rapid rate, and the 7th began to
show great promise. Davidson's hopes for the regimental command completely disappeared when, on
November 1, 1866, he received orders to assume duties
as Acting Inspector-General of the Department of Missouri, after the arrival of the, to be designated, commander of the 7th. On November 23, General Order
No. 92 was issued by the War Department. That order
formally established the 7th Cavalry Regiment as of
September 21, 1866, naming Colonel Andrew J. Smith
as commander, and Lieutenant Colonel George A.
Custer as second in command. Naturally the appointment of Custer to the rank of lieutenant colonel was an
item of considerable concern to Davidson. And, no
wonder. Custer was some twenty years his junior, only
about six years out of West Point, and possessed of a far
less illustrious war record. Nevertheless Davidson retained command of the 7th until Colonel Smith arrived
on November 26, regardless of the fact that Custer had
reported to Fort Riley on November 3, 1866.

The new assignment, Acting Inspector-General of
the department, was a choice one. Since it was a position
normally filled by a colonel, Davidson felt hopeful that
it indicated his future status. As soon as Colonel Smith
assumed command of the 7th, Davidson and his family
moved to Fort Leavenworth, where the Departmental
Commander, General Hancock, and his staff were
housed. It is interesting to note, at this juncture, that this
change in assignment as well as the one with the 7th
Cavalry, did not alter Davidson's relationship with the
Second Cavalry. He remained as the commander of the

2nd, on detached duty. Such detached assignments were quite common for a great many years after the Civil War ended. During those years regimental officers were frequently given detached duty assignments for as long as two to three years, then returned to their regiments. After his arrival in Fort Leavenworth, Davidson became so immersed in a multitude of inspections at the numerous posts under General Hancock's command, that he had little time to think about the results of the Selection Board. As time permitted he glanced at selection lists as soon as possible after they were published, but his name never appeared, and it began to look as though he had been passed over.

One day Davidson noted that an opening existed for a lieutenant colonel in the newly formed Tenth Cavalry Regiment. He lost no time in applying for that position. Highly favorable endorsements and other excellent recommendations were helpful in having his request approved without delay. However, there was a catch to it. Two of the four new cavalry regiments that had been authorized were designated to be all Negro, with white officers, on an experimental basis. Although Negro organizations had performed well during the war, they were in the infantry. There was a great deal of doubt that they could perform equally as well as white men in mounted units. Therefore, it was concluded that the success of the Negro cavalrymen depended upon the caliber of their officers. In order to insure the best possible officer structure, the policy was established that each officer must be carefully screened before his assignment to one of the Negro cavalry regiments. The screening criterion was that each officer must have a distinguished Civil War record, and be examined in person by a review board especially created for the purpose. Davidson was well qualified on his war record, so no time was lost in arranging his appearance before the board. He learned that his Virginia ancestry, and the fact that he grew up in that state, were decided assets. This background gave him a degree of tolerance for Negroes that was superior to most Northerners, and he understood them. Therefore, he received the appointment as Lieutenant Colonel, Tenth U.S. Cavalry, on December 1, 1866.

Although not destined to join his regiment for several years, Davidson took a keen interest in it from the first day of his assignment to it. The Tenth was being formed in Fort Riley, not far from Fort Leavenworth, which made it easy to keep a close eye on its progress. The fact that he was on the staff of the Departmental Commander was an added asset. He, therefore, did all possible to give the regiment a good start. It was then that he became acquainted with the commander of the Tenth, Colonel Benjamin H. Grierson. He soon learned that Grierson had no military background and, since he had been a civilian prior to the war, was very vague on army administrative procedures. Grierson's background was that he had been a small town music teacher who enlisted at the outbreak of the war. He was assigned, as a private, to a volunteer cavalry regiment from Illinois. Having better than an average education he rose rapidly and at the end of his first year became regimental commander with the brevet rank of colonel. His one claim to fame occurred when, on April 18, 1863, he led a cavalry expedition, known as Grierson's Raid, into the deep South, to assist General Grant in his assault on, and capture of, Vicksburg. From that time onward Grierson was one of Grant's favorites. It was Grant who personally directed that Grierson be given command of the Tenth, and so far as can be determined without being required to appear before the review board. When this became known a wave of bitterness swept through a great many intermediate-grade career officers who desired such a command, knowing themselves to be better qualified and yet relegated to lower ranks.

Although Davidson was upset to learn of Grierson's appointment, especially when he found that Grierson would be his regimental commander, he did not permit it to affect his loyalty to the army. And, since the Tenth was now his regiment, he smothered his feelings under a firm resolve to help Grierson in every possible way. He, therefore, made such an offer and it was gladly accepted. What Davidson did not learn, until a few years later, was that Grierson's inexperience also motivated him to rely very heavily upon his staff and other officers of the regiment for guidance in the day-to-day administrative and procedural matters. In return he felt obligated to them, and became unusually tolerant of their numerous infractions of dress, deportment and discipline standards. It is suspected that some of those officers took an unfair advantage of their standing with the colonel. All this, of course, was anathema to any field-grade officer of the regular army.

In considering the foregoing it seems appropriate at this time to examine the philosophy of the regular officers of that era, relative to the prevailing system of appointments and promotions. It is neatly summed up in the following quotation from the *Centennial of the U.S. Military Academy, 1802-1902,*

At the end of 40 years (after establishment of West Point) there were but 5 graduates above the rank of captain of the line. After the close of the Civil War there was not more than 1 grad. to every 10 officers in the infantry and cavalry, which did about all the Indian campaigning. These matters must be considered in giving the story of Indian Wars where West Point men have borne a hand. What share their sons have taken in other fields is another story.

It was nearly 60 years before a graduate of the Academy reached the full grade of General of the line. When McClellan was made a General the Military Academy had graduated nearly 2,000 men, and McClellan, by the way, was appointed from civil life. In that period of 60 years 37 men who began their military careers, from civil life, after the installation of the Military Academy reached the full grade of General of the line, and three of them were President of the United States. Why did this institution fail to breed a single general in all those years filled with warfare? The reason is that military experience and knowledge were not usually essential qualities for that position. Let us look at that list. Twenty-three out of 37 generals were practically without military experience; of the remaining 14 all but 3 entered the service at the grade of captain or higher. Some of them were undoubtedly fine soldiers, but so were hundreds of others who did not get so fair a start. It is not so hard to reach high rank when you begin at a point which other men take many years to reach. The graduates of West Point entered as 2nd Lieutenants and Brevet 2nd Lieutenants, and by the time they attained the rank from which selections are made they were old and worn out. The record of Indian Wars is a history of the deeds of Captains and Lieutenants, for the most part, many of whom were killed and disabled, after showing the highest military qualities. So that West Pointers in Indian Wars, in addition to the hardships of the service, saw themselves in a class that was barred from the high rewards of their profession, by men who entered at a higher rank and at an early age from civil life.

In addition to the aforementioned McClellan, even more famous generals who attained high rank during the Civil War were,

1. U.S. Grant – West Point class 1843. In 1854 was given the choice of a court-martial or resigning from the army because of his addiction to alcohol. Returned to the army in 1861 in rank of colonel.
2. H. W. Halleck – West Point graduate who resigned in 1854. Re-entered the army in 1861 as major general.
3. W. T. Sherman – West Point class 1840. In 1853, in rank of captain, resigned. Returned to the army with the rank of colonel in 1861.

Regardless of the fact that those officers distinguished themselves during the war, it is difficult to understand how they could be considered superior, at the time of re-entry, to a host of career officers who had been on continuous active duty for twenty or more years, and eager to achieve comparable ranks and commands.

Had it not been for the deeply rooted philosophy of a host of career officers, as outlined in the "Centennial" quotation, the officer corps might have shattered when the final Selection Board results were published. One incident, above all others, almost did it. That was the appointment of Custer to the lieutenant colonel's position in the 7th Cavalry. The majority of these officers considered him to be an upstart. Much has been written about Custer, and there is no need for reviewing it here.[3] There is one area not generally covered in those publications, and that is the results of a psychiatric analysis made by Dr. Karl Menninger, and published in a 1947 issue of the *Journal of the American Medical Association.* To quote that eminent psychiatrist,

> Custer is a personality type only too familiar to Psychiatrists, falling into a category of Psychopathology characterized by excessive vanity, either to the principles of humanity or to the established code of ethics.

---

[3] An understanding of the effect of Custer on career officers can be gleaned from F. F. Van de Water, *Glory Hunter;* and Richard Wormser, *Yellowlegs.*

Paraphrasing other sections of that analysis, Menninger classified Custer as a man who executed surprise attacks, with overwhelming superiority of forces, upon Indian communities, and indiscriminately slaughtered men, women and children. He utterly disregarded the safety of his troops, and sent them into hostilities without sufficient preparation. He would deliberately sacrifice the lives of his command in order to achieve a small measure of glory.

The foregoing reference to Custer is included because his actions during ensuing years had a profound effect upon the military commanders who were responsible for prosecuting the Indian Wars. It is this writer's opinion that the Indian problem could have been solved much easier, had it not been for Custer.

About the first of June 1867, Davidson, in response to a directive from General Hancock, set out to make an inspection of the only two military posts in the Oklahoma Territory, Fort Gibson and Fort Arbuckle. The purpose of the mission was to determine the adequacy of those forts to accommodate the additional cavalry and infantry troops the general planned to move into the territory. Davidson assembled a staff, twenty-five Indian Scouts, and a twenty-man troop from the Tenth Cavalry, commanded by Lieutenant R. H. Pratt, for the expedition. They left Fort Leavenworth via rail for St. Louis where a river steamer provided transportation to Memphis, then another steamer on the White River to the nearest railhead, by rail to Little Rock, and finally a steamer on the Arkansas River to Fort Gibson. No time was lost in making an inspection of that fort, and preparing for the journey to Fort Arbuckle, some two hundred miles west. That last stage turned out to be far more of a contest of endurance than anyone had anticipated. Their route was by horseback over very rough terrain, and through heavily forested areas, in weather that was beastly hot.

A few days after leaving Fort Gibson, Davidson became ill. The circumstances are best described in the following report of the staff surgeon, Brevet Major Van Buren Hubbard, on August 10, 1867,

> I hereby certify that on the twenty second day of June I left this Fort [Gibson] to accompany Major General John W. Davidson on a tour of inspection of Fort Arbuckle, C.N. [Cherokee Nation] about two hundred miles distant; that the weather was exceedingly, though not unusually, warm for the latitude and season; that we had made about eighty-five miles when General Davidson was so overcome by the heat as to render it extremely hazardous, in my opinion, for him to prosecute the journey further; and by my advice he turned back and returned to his post by easy stages, traveling during the cool of the morning and evening only; that his symptoms were those of one who had previously suffered a sunstroke.
>
> I hereby declare my opinion and belief that service in a Southern latitude would seriously involve the health of General Davidson, if not actually endanger his life.

Before starting the return journey General Davidson appointed the chief quartermaster, Brevet Major Amos S. Kimball, to carry on with the inspection of Fort Arbuckle. The return to Fort Leavenworth was accomplished in time to arrive shortly after September first.

Upon his return to Fort Leavenworth, General Davidson was appointed to membership on a General Court-Martial Board, under Special Order No. 426, dated August 27, 1867. The order was issued by the adjutant general's office, by the order of the Commanding General U.S. Army, General U.S. Grant. The composition of the court, in order of their seniority, was,[4]

1. Brevet Major General Wm. Hoffman; Colonel, Third U.S. Infantry.
2. Brevet Major General John W. Davidson; Lieutenant Colonel, Tenth U.S. Cavalry.
3. Brevet Major General Benjamin H. Grierson; Colonel, Tenth U.S. Cavalry.
4. Brevet Brigadier General Pitcairn Morrison; Colonel, U.S. Army (Retired).
5. Brevet Brigadier General Michael R. Morgan; Major, Commissary of Subsistence.
6. Brevet Brigadier General Franklin D. Callender; Lieutenant Colonel, Ordnance Department.
7. Brevet Lieutenant Colonel Thomas C. English; Major, Fifth U.S. Infantry.
8. Brevet Major Henry Ashbury; Captain, Third U.S. Infantry.
9. Brevet Major Stephen C. Lyford; Captain, Ordnance Department.
10. Brevet Lieutenant Colonel Robert Chandler; Captain, Thirteenth U.S. Infantry, judge advocate of the court.

The court was directed to convene September 15, 1867, at 11 a.m. to try, by general court-martial, Lieutenant Colonel George A. Custer, Seventh U.S. Cavalry, on three charges and eight specifications. One charge accused Custer of leaving his command at a time when it was supposed to engage hostile Indians (absent without leave from his command). The second charge accused him of using regimental personnel and equipment for his own private purposes. The third charge was for alleged cruelty to certain personnel, and directing that deserters from his regiment be hunted down and shot.

---

[4] Quotations and statements concerning the Custer court-martial are from the proceedings of the court-martial, and repeated in Lawrence A. Frost, *The Court-Martial of General George Armstrong Custer.*

Prior to beginning the trial two of the junior officers had a disagreement over their rank and precedence on the court. The dispute was submitted to the convening authority, who ruled that the rank and precedence of all members of the court was assigned in accordance with the seniority of their highest brevet ranks. From that ruling, it is interesting to note that Davidson out-ranked his regimental commander, Colonel Grierson, while serving on the court. Once that problem was settled another sprang up. The counsel for the defense, Lieutenant Colonel C. C. Parsons, presented, on behalf of Custer, an objection to Davidson's membership on the court. Custer alleged that Davidson was a material witness in the case and would, therefore, be prejudiced against Custer. The objection was overruled by the court. The defense counsel again objected, on the basis that Davidson had been heard making this remark,

> I do not see how General Custer expected to get out of these charges. He is a young man – a newcomer to the service – he only graduated in '61, and never commanded a company, and he must be taught that he cannot come out here and do as he pleases.

The pent-up feelings of Davidson and a host of other army officers certainly came to the surface with that statement. As the Court started to retire for considera-tion of this objection the defense counsel added,

> Davidson and the Judge Advocate of the Court occupy the same office, and that might further prejudice Davidson's position on the Court.

In an effort to satisfy everyone concerned Davidson said,

> I know of nothing at the present time that would incapacitate me from sitting as a fair and impartial member of this Court, but on the general principle of desiring the accused to be satisfied in his own mind of the impartiality of the proceedings I desire to be excused from sitting on the case.

After due deliberation, in closed court, the court decided to grant Davidson's request, and relieved him of membership on the court.

Since the charges and specifications were so serious the trial proceedings moved along very slowly. On October 11, 1867, the court announced that Custer had been found guilty on all charges and specifications, and sentenced, "to be suspended from rank and command for one year and to forfeit his pay proper for the same time." The proceedings, findings and sentence were approved at all command levels, and forwarded to the Bureau of Military Justice for final action. On November 8, 1867, the Bureau passed it on to the Secretary of War, General Grant, for approval. In his endorsement Grant said, among other things,

> The proceedings, findings and sentence in the case of Brevet Major General Custer are approved. The levity of the sentence, considering the nature of the offense of Brevet Major General Custer if found guilty, is to be remarked on.

It is to be noted that reviewing and approving authorities, of a court-martial case, are empowered to mitigate a sentence, but have no power to increase it. Consequently, those remarks of Grant constituted a severe reprimand to all members of the court, for their extreme leniency.

Quite some time before Custer's year of suspension expired, General Sheridan, a very good friend of the Custers, prevailed upon Generals Sherman and Grant to have Custer reinstated. According to Sheridan, Custer was the only man capable of leading a planned operation against the Indians. He had his way, and Custer returned to full duty status on September 24, 1868, and rejoined the Seventh Cavalry. Sheridan's plan was to move against the Indians, who were thought to be concentrated in large numbers in the Washita Mountains. He had chosen the Seventh Cavalry for the task, at a time when it was temporarily commanded by a junior, Major Elliott, during Colonel Smith's absence on detached duty. Presumably other commanders and troops could not be made available for that expedition.

As it turned out there was but one group, consisting of about two hundred warriors, women and children encamped in the mountains at the time. The chief of this group, Black Kettle, happened to be one who was well known to be friendly to the whites. All this was reported to Custer by his scouts. Nevertheless he swooped down on Black Kettle's camp, very early in the morning of a bitterly cold day in late November 1868. The Indians did not have a chance against that force of nearly seven hundred troopers, and all but fifty or sixty women and children were killed. That act spurred the Indians to greatly increase their hostilities throughout the Plains areas.

In June of 1868 Davidson received orders to a newly created post. It was to be Professor of Military Science and Tactics at the State Agricultural College, in Manhattan, Kansas. This post came into being as a result of a move, on the part of the authorities in Washington, designed to prepare a military reserve force in a few selected colleges. This was a way of being prepared for the increasing Indian hostilities without increasing the size of the army, even though it was much below its authorized strength. All male students were to be required to take military training, some of whom would become junior officers when called up.

The college at Manhattan was the first of the selected

schools to implement the program, and the burden fell upon Davidson to develop the course of instruction. The *History of the Kansas State College of Agriculture and Applied Science,* published in 1940, covers the program as follows,

> Lieut. Col. J. W. Davidson, of the United States Cavalry was detailed by General Grant to be professor of military tactics. He had been Brevetted a major general, and was habitually addressed and referred to as "General Davidson." He entered with spirit and sincerity upon his work at the College, and introduced an elaborate course of military subjects. All physically fit male students were required to take military drill, and other military features that might be selected.

In addition to his military duties Davidson accepted an offer to become professor of civil engineering, and to teach French and Spanish. That gave him a full schedule, but he seemed to thrive on hard work and took it all in stride. That complete change from rigorous life on a military post was, indeed, a welcome change. Soon after arriving in Manhattan he bought a home on a small hill on the outskirts of the town. It remained as the family home for many years, a place for them to enjoy when on a leave of absence or between duty assignments.

It had been the fervent hope of all the Davidsons that the climate in Manhattan would be beneficial to his health. But that was not to be for Davidson. During the summer following his arrival in Manhattan he suffered two severe bouts with the old malarial condition. At times he had to muster all of his iron determination in order to carry on with the college duties. Finally, believing that his health would not permit a return to active service in the field, he initiated a request to the

Adjutant General, to be ordered before a "Retiring Board." The request was dated August 9, 1869, and submitted in accordance with the provision of "Section 16, Retirement Act of August 3, 1861." He cited as reasons the numerous malarial attacks which began with the sunstroke in mid-1862. Shortly after his request left in the mail, a letter arrived which indicated the retired list to be full. Davidson immediately dispatched another letter requesting that his retirement request be deferred until vacancies occurred on the retired list.

One year later Davidson learned that a few vacancies existed on the retired list; therefore, under date of July 14, 1870, he asked that his original request be reinstated. Special Order No. 194, dated August 9, 1870, signed by General Townsend, convened a board to consider requests for retirement. That board met on August 17, 1870, at Fort Leavenworth, Kansas, and Davidsons' request was placed before it.

Davidson was called, by the board, on November 9, 1870. Lieutenant Henry Jackson, Seventh Cavalry, served as recorder. Certificates from nine different army surgeons were introduced by Davidson, all of which attested to his frequent bouts with malaria, especially in hot weather. Along with those certificates, numerous pertinent documents from the adjutant general's office were read into the record. Next the board instructed the two surgeon members of the board to give Davidson a thorough physical examination, then adjourned until the next day. On November 10 the board re-convened, and the surgeons submitted their report, which concluded with,

We have been unable to discover anything that would prevent him from performing all the duties of an officer. The fact of his

having suffered isolation we do not consider sufficient to prevent
him from performing his duty in the field, inasmuch as the cause
of his malady appears to be increased temperature of the body,
particularly when a person is much fatigued. We deem it easy for
an officer to adopt such means as will keep the head cool, and by
drinking enough water to keep the body from being overheated.

Davidson rebutted by calling the board's attention to
the several certifications from different surgeons which
attested to his malarian condition. All of those certificates were similar in tone to the one quoted earlier in
this chapter, written by Surgeon Van Buren Hubbard,
on August 10, 1867. He then asked one question, "Do
you think a person is any more sensitive to the heat of
the sun because he has once received an Ictussolis?" The
senior surgeon replied,

I would not say that a person could not have it a second time, but
I cannot recall any other case in my life where a person has had a
second attack, except this one, there appears to be a great deal of
nervous excitability in this case.

Davidson made one more brief plea to the board, in
which he again cited the numerous medical certificates,
and described the attacks that had occurred since the
first one in 1862. In conclusion he said,

I do not assert that I am physically unable to perform the ordi-
nary duties of an officer of my rank in time of peace, but I do
believe that like exposure to the heat of the sun in warm weather
would produce like dangerous results, and that I am peculiarly
sensitive to its effects from my former injury.

The case was closed and the board briefly considered
the evidence and testimony. Then, under date of November 10, 1870, wrote its report and recommendation,
concluding with,

The Board, after having maturely considered the evidence addressed to the Board, is unable to find anything that would incapacitate Lieut. Col. John W. Davidson, 10th regiment U.S. Cavalry, for active service.

By that disapproval the board effectively closed the door on any future retirement proceedings for Davidson, unless some new disability occurred.[5]

Upon learning of the action of the board, General Sherman, General-in-Chief of the Army, sent a telegram to Davidson, dated November 21, 1870, expressing sympathy. The entire tone of the message was one of a concerned friend, and he mentioned that one possible solution might be a resignation. Davidson replied with thanks, and said that any thought of resignation was out of the question, since all his training had been in the army and he was ill-equipped to compete with civilians for suitable employment. He concluded his remarks with a statement, saying, "I prefer to join my regiment. Nothing could induce me to resign after nearly twenty-five years' service."

At this juncture this writer would like to inject some personal observations about the proceedings of the retiring board. The emphasis placed upon the physical examination of Davidson by the medical members of the board, appears to be unwarranted. The board convened on November 9, and completed action on the case the following day. Certainly, therefore, the physical examination could not have been more than cursory. And these proceedings occurred in November when the weather was quite cold, a period of any year when Davidson's health happened to be good. His entire medical history shows one attack after another, during

---

[5] The entire proceedings of the retirement board are contained in the Davidson ACP file. Quotations and statements used herein are from that source.

hot and humid weather. By their action the board certified that Davidson was completely fit, and able to perform duty under any climatic situation. Davidson was plagued with intermittent bouts of malaria throughout the remainder of his life.

When the retirement board proceedings ended it became evident to Davidson that his remaining time in Manhattan would be limited. That was manifested by the vast increase in the activities of army units in the plains areas, to combat the rapidly growing number of hostile Indian attacks. It was no surprise, therefore, when in early December of 1870, information reached him that he would soon join his regiment. The actual date of his transfer depended upon finding a suitable replacement. As it developed an officer of appropriate rank and suitability could not be spared from service in the field, and the reserves could not supply a qualified individual. As a consequence army headquarters decided to suspend college training activities until the demands for officers in the field decreased. Davidson was directed to phase out the military activities at the earliest possible date, which he did by the end of the year. It was eleven years before the military science and tactics program was reinstated in the Kansas State Agricultural College.

7

Oklahoma and Indians

Once the military training activities at the college were closed down Lieutenant Colonel Davidson moved quickly to his newly-assigned post of duty. He was directed to take command of Camp Supply, Indian Territory. Shortly after the turn of the new year, 1871, he arrived and relieved Lieutenant Colonel A. D. Nelson, 3rd U.S. Infantry, who had been the camp commander for quite some time. There were four companies of the Tenth Cavalry, commanded by Major M. N. Kidd, and approximately the same number of infantry troops stationed there at the time. The headquarters for Colonel Grierson and the Tenth Cavalry was then at Fort Sill, Indian Territory. Grierson also commanded that fort. Davidson found out immediately that the cavalry troops were unusually low in morale, a condition that had been growing for many months. It started in the early spring of 1870 when they bore the brunt of the increasingly savage and frequent attacks of the Kiowa Indians. Although the cavalry constituted about one-half of the total strength of the garrison they believed that they had been ineptly deployed, assigned missions that should have been fulfilled by infantry, and had suffered severe maulings by the Indians because of poor equipment and incompetent leadership. The cavalrymen did not, however, blame their misfortunes on Major Kidd, since they stoutly maintained that Colonel Nelson was at fault for using the cavalry in such a manner that they faced unnecessarily hazardous situations.

The poor equipment factor was real, involving insufficient ammunition, antiquated carbines, horses that had been cast off from other units, and sub-standard saddles. It was evident that the 7th Cavalry was being furnished with the choice equipment and animals. The situation was summed up, very angrily, by Captain Carter, commanding H Company, Tenth Cavalry, in a letter to Colonel Grierson, dated May 22, 1870, in which he said,

> The Tenth has been getting mean, and worn out horses of the 7th Cavalry. Many of these nags died within days of reaching this post. Since our first mount in 1867 this regiment has received nothing but broken down horses and repaired equipment, as I am willing to testify to as far as my knowledge goes.

It is obvious that this was a continuation of the discrimination that had been practiced against the Negro troopers from the very beginning. In spite of those handicaps the troopers of the Tenth gave an excellent account of themselves in almost every encounter with the Indians. When Davidson, a tried and true cavalryman, took command of the post the cavalrymen of the garrison received a big morale boost. They felt that since their new commander understood their problems he would provide the type of leadership that was completely lacking under Colonel Nelson.[1] In addition the Negro troopers especially appreciated the new commander because he was a Virginian, and as such would understand the problems that were peculiar to black men far more readily than one who was raised in the

---

[1] See Robert C. Carriker, *Fort Supply, Indian Territory;* and Donald J. Berthong, *The Southern Cheyennes.*

North. It is said that, on the night of Davidson's assumption of command, the officers and men of the Tenth toasted their new commander long and generously in the several parties that were held in the barracks and quarters. Although Davidson was a strict disciplinarian, he probably overlooked the bleary eyes that filled the ranks at assembly the following morning.

Before proceeding further, a review of the peculiar problems that faced the officers of the Ninth and Tenth Cavalry, seems appropriate. As mentioned earlier, the experiment of developing Negroes into good cavalrymen was, in most of the higher levels, viewed with great misgivings. Nevertheless, the rapidly increasing hostility of the Plains Indians emphasized the need for making them effective enough to carry their full share of the burden that was placed upon the army. Hence the necessity for carefully screening the officers who would train, then lead them into battle. Their foe, the Plains Indians, were ranked by some authorities as superior to the very best cavalry troops in Europe. The Sioux, Cheyennes and Comanches were indeed excellent horsemen, comparable to the Mongols or Cossacks. General George Crook once said, "The Sioux is a cavalry soldier from the time he has intelligence enough to ride a horse or fire a gun." Another experienced cavalry officer is reputed to have said,

> They are the finest light cavalry in the world. The Sioux of the Northern Plains were far more to be dreaded than any European cavalry.

Since the success of the Negro regiments hinged entirely upon the caliber of each officer so assigned, the selection of regimental officers could not be a perfunctory operation, nor in accordance with the customary army routine. The criterion established was that the officers from the rank of captain and higher would be, two-thirds from the volunteer cavalry and one-third from regular cavalry, all of whom must have distinguished records. All junior officers, from second lieutenant on up, had to have better than average records. Those requirements established eligibility for appearance before the selection board. The net result was that both regiments came into being with excellent officers. Time proved that to be an extremely sound policy, as demonstrated by the outstanding performance of both regiments in skirmishes against hostile Indians during the ensuing twenty years.

Under the attitudes prevailing in many factions of the army, and the public, the Negro troopers were horribly discriminated against, and little credit was given for their bravery under fire. History records numerous outstanding accomplishments by the cavalry, during the Plains Indian Wars, but little credit was given to the Negro troopers. In fact, either inferentially or directly, much of the credit for their accomplishments was given to all-white regiments. Certainly, therefore, the officers who accepted those assignments had fortitude, interest in, and dedication to their jobs. Without these attributes they could not have succeeded, because the problems they faced had never before been encountered by the U.S. Cavalry. Many of the newly recruited troopers were just a short time out of the bonds of slavery, very few could read and write, and the vast majority were illiterate. As a consequence it became the practice to appoint those who could read and write, no matter how little, to the positions of corporal and sergeant. Even so, most of the duties involving paperwork of any description, had to be done by the officers – work which was usually performed by non-coms in the white regiments. Years of painstaking effort were required of all officers to convert these men into effective cavalrymen. It is a great tribute to the caliber of the officers in those regiments that their extraordinary efforts eventually produced two crack cavalry regiments.

For several years after the Ninth and Tenth Regiments were formed they faced serious problems in finding enough recruits to fill their complements. In the beginning everyone thought that since most of the men would be coming from the southern plantations, they would eagerly accept the $13.00 monthly pay of a soldier. It was also, optimistically, thought that many of those who had performed well as infantrymen during the war would gladly join the cavalry units. As it turned out, however, most of those ex-infantrymen had little or no experience with horses, and were reluctant to switch to the mounted regiments. Consequently it required a vigorous campaign to find willing recruits, and ex-soldiers who were agreeable to be trained as cavalrymen. Characteristic of the attitude then prevalent among the Negroes is the story of a recruiter in New York City who approached a likely-looking young Negro and asked if he would like to join. The Negro said that he would gladly join the infantry, but not the cavalry. When asked why, he replied, "Wal suh – if dat genrl evah holler retreat, I doan wanta be bothered with no horse."

Those who did join the cavalry were, for the most part, ignorant, not self-reliant, unaccustomed to cleanliness, knew nothing about the care of horses and equipment, but they did want to learn. All instruction and drill had to be done by the officers, whereas their counterparts in white regiments had the strong and expert assistance of non-commissioned officers. It was soon learned that group instruction quite often had to be supplemented by individual instruction. Almost every man had to be taught personal hygiene, weapons care and handling, equipment maintenance and the care of horses. Extreme patience was essential because the learning process was much slower than with white recruits.

Although the regiment had been in existence for nearly four years at the time Davidson joined it, an enormous amount of hard work still remained before Negro troopers could hold their own with their white counterparts. And, of course, discrimination was the most difficult problem of all. Obviously that had been practiced with the soldiers of the Tenth, who were stationed at Camp Supply. Hence there was good cause for the Negroes to rejoice when Davidson took command, but the white infantrymen had a different reaction. That was summed up in the memoirs of Captain Richard T. Jacob, 6th U.S. Infantry,[2] who was serving as a second lieutenant when Davidson took command of Camp Supply. He wrote,

> Davidson was not popular, his petulance and favoritism did not make for good harmony and discipline in the garrison.

As in all situations, it all depends upon which side a person is on, because the officers of the Tenth Cavalry at the post, and the Indian Agent, Darlington, voiced this sentiment,[3]

---

[2] *Chronicles of Oklahoma,* vol. 2, no. 1.   [3] Carriker, *Fort Supply.*

The tensions lessened when Lieut. Col. J. W. Davidson, Tenth Cavalry, replaced Lieut. Col. Nelson as commanding officer at Camp Supply.

As a matter of fact Darlington had previously taken action to have a strong military leader assigned, who would move to control the hostile Indian activity in the area. In the request he originated he said, "Some discreet and capable person to be sent to bring the Cheyenne warriors under control." Darlington's request was prompted by the almost constant vacillation of Colonel Nelson, and his bickering with the Indian agent. At one point Nelson had written that he did not want the agent to have full jurisdiction over the Indians in the area because "The Cheyennes will behave themselves, but if they do it will be from fear of punishment alone." [4] This contrasted with his attitude when Darlington first arrived at Camp Supply, when Nelson insisted that the agent was solely responsible. Within a month he claimed that, until the Indians were actually on their reservation, the army had complete control over them. Thus the argument raged back and forth, without a meeting of the minds. This was the messy situation facing Lieutenant Colonel Davidson when he arrived at Camp Supply. One of Davidson's first acts, upon assuming command of the post, was to evaluate the prevailing situation, then reverse his predecessor's policy of not allowing an Indian upon the post. That change of policy permitted chiefs, who were well disposed, to visit the post commander in his headquarters when they had problems to discuss. As a consequence of that single change, the atmosphere began to improve and soon the post commander and the Indian Agent were cooperating fully.

---

[4] *Ibid.*

The controversy with the Indian Agent was only part of the awkward situation that faced Davidson. Another one was that the camp was detested by nearly everyone, the wives in particular. It was situated in a barren area, far from any form of civilization, with a climate that seemed miserable most of the time. The quarters for both men and officers were made of cottonwood logs, with mud used in lieu of plaster to seal cracks, and leakage during wet weather was commonplace. The officers' family quarters were similarly constructed, with dirt or sand floors, and wall partitions of canvas. Bugs and insects thrived in the wooden walls, and snakes had the uncanny ability to enter the shacks at will. That was a severe shock to the wives of junior officers, who were often fresh from aristocratic and comfortable homes in the East. Their visions of a glamorous life as wives of army officers were soon shattered. The colonel's lady, Clara Davidson, who arrived with her husband, soon took her rightful place as the post commander's wife. Fortunately she had "roughed it" many years earlier, in New Mexico and California, and knew how to cope with such conditions. She soon restored order among the female population, and got them interested in many different projects. Although this could not eliminate their feelings of revulsion, it did serve to relieve their tensions and help them to adjust to the environment. One lieutenant's wife wrote in a letter to her parents,

> This country itself is bad enough, and the location of the post is most unfortunate, but to compel officers and men to live in these old huts of decaying, moldy wood, which are reeking with malaria and alive with bugs, and perhaps snakes, is wicked.

One of the basic requirements for all the women at

Camp Supply was to spend enough time on the target range to qualify with the carbine, and 45-caliber pistol. Usually they carried pocket derringers, and were thoroughly imbued with the necessity for killing their children and themselves if faced with capture by the Indians. To illustrate the tense situation prevailing at Camp Supply during 1872 and 1873, Private H. Harbers, 3rd U.S. Infantry, wrote his parents as follows,

> The post sustained repeated raids, and the men became accustomed to maintaining a state of readiness. Contact with the Indians was frequent, and we would lie down behind windows with cartridges strewn over the floor. Sentries were subject to persistent sneak attacks by prowling enemies. At 8:30 one night I went to the farthest end of my beat to exchange the situation with the next guard. When I got there he did not report, so I roused the Corporal of the Guard. They hunted and found him in the haystack with two arrows in his neck. Fortunately he recovered.

As was characteristic of the army posts on the frontier, the enlisted men's wives and daughters often served as housemaids and laundresses for the officers in order to earn extra money. It is indeed a tribute to American womanhood that most of the army wives were truly devoted and loyal to their husbands. With the utmost fortitude they adjusted to the constant danger of living in the many small garrisons that were usually surrounded by hostile Indians. That they also took up rifles to assist in defending these garrisons from Indian attacks, is a fact that is not well known. When a husband was transferred from one post to another, his family would accompany him, if there was a supply wagon train. Wives and children usually rode in the ambulances as they covered countless miles through hostile Indian territory. What a blessing it must have been when, several years later, most of those army posts were connected by rail lines.

Entertainment at the frontier posts consisted of dinner parties, balls, masquerades, picnics, and amateur theatricals. At most of these affairs the regimental bands would burst forth with their finest music. At other times the bands gave frequent concerts. One can safely assume that life on some of those posts would have been extremely dull without a band. Single girls on those posts were very much in demand for dances and parties. And since there was always a great demand for wives by the bachelor officers, the single girls often married at very young ages. Among the wives, however, there were always a few malcontents who could not adjust to a life so far away from civilization. Some of them packed up and moved back to their homes in the East. Most of these would make life such a living hell for their husbands that some men simply gave up and resigned. The army lost plenty of excellent officers in this manner. Another problem that contributed to the difficulty of living in a frontier post, was the scarcity of living quarters. Assignment to these quarters was always on the basis of seniority. Whenever a new, and comparatively senior, officer arrived with his family there would be a large scale reshuffling of quarters. That actually was a bumping operation that went all the way down the line, causing numerous moves. The "low men on the totem pole," second lieutenants, generally bore the brunt of such a shuffle, and sometimes wound up in tents, along with their wives and children. Not infrequently, quarrels broke out, especially among the women involved, which would strain the social relationships for some weeks thereafter.

Probably one of the most difficult problems for the wives to solve was that of cooking. Kitchen equipment was wholly inadequate, crude, and difficult to keep clean. Food supplies were not always of good quality – the flour was generally full of weevils, beef usually tough and stringy, and milk was usually thin and watery. Refrigeration depended upon the amount of ice that could be cut and stored in the winter, for use during the summer. Most generally the storage facilities for ice were limited and crude, therefore it was a genuine treat in mid-summer to sit down with any kind of iced drink. None of these problems were strange to Mrs. Davidson, since she had experienced all of them in the far West, prior to the Civil War. She made herself available to all the women of the post to help them to cope with what, to them, seemed hopeless situations. She gave generously of her time and energy in helping the women to prepare tasty meals out of the poor foodstuffs that were hardly fit for use. As mentioned earlier, she became an excellent cook, especially under adverse conditions, and passed this knowledge along. That, together with her motherly nature, endeared her to the female population of all her husband's posts of duty.

In the beginning of 1871 the intensity of the hostile Indian attacks increased sharply, with many of them arising in the vicinity of Fort Sill, which was the headquarters of the Tenth Cavalry. The commander of the post, and the Tenth Cavalry, Colonel Grierson, endeavored to help solve the most difficult problems by seeking the advice of the departmental commander, General Sherman. Ultimately, the general decided to see the situation at first hand. He set up a meeting between himself, Colonel Grierson, and the local Indian

Agent, Tatum. He arrived at Fort Sill on May 23, 1871, and issued an invitation to the Kiowa chiefs to come in for a series of talks. In one of the resulting sessions one of the chiefs, Satanta, became belligerent and accused the agent of cheating the Indians, and demanded guns and ammunition. He also bragged that he, and Chiefs Satank and Big Tree, had led a big raid, a few weeks earlier, on a large wagon train near Jacksboro, Texas, which became a massacre. Upon hearing this Sherman called a private conference, in the colonel's quarters, where it was decided to arrest the guilty Indians. The chiefs were then summoned and informed that they were under arrest and would be sent to Texas for trial.

Meanwhile, the Cheyennes in the vicinity of Camp Supply were relatively peaceful. But their activities were a constant source of worry to both Davidson and Darlington. During all this time the two worked closely together in an effort to maintain peace, which was jittery at best. For many years in the Great Plains areas, the major responsibility for Indian affairs was in the hands of Indian agents. Most of these men were Quakers, who were pacific in nature and prone to rely too heavily upon the word of the Indian chiefs. This division of authority operated to deprive the military commanders of the freedom to do what they thought best for the interests of all concerned. Usually, therefore, strained relations between post commanders and Indian agents became the order of the day. That situation was the cause of considerable worry to Colonel Grierson. He complained constantly to the authorities in Washington, who seemed to be oblivious to the problem. On the other hand, during that period of strife, much credit was due to both Darlington and Davidson for the cooperative manner in which they handled Indian problems in the vicinity of Camp Supply. Certainly that remark does not suggest that all Indian problems were eliminated in the area, as that would have been impossible. But their frequency and intensity did tend to decrease after Davidson assumed command of the post. Eventually the complaints of such commanders as Grierson, and the general increase of Indian uprisings, in late 1871, brought about a policy change which gave the military more authority. Thereafter they were entitled to enter the reservations in pursuit of offenders, to make appropriate arrests, and to conduct periodic inspections – something that had been prohibited for several years.

As the tempo of military activities increased the peaceful, or near peaceful conditions in the vicinity of Camp Supply began to deteriorate in spite of the best efforts of the camp commander and the Indian agent. The relatives of Satanta and Santank, who lived in the area, decided to get revenge for the arrests of their kinsmen by Sherman and Grierson. The intensity and ferocity of the Indian hostilities began to increase rapidly. An added irritant to the military was a new influx of whiskey peddlers and unscrupulous traders, who crossed the border from Kansas to supply "fire-water" and firearms to the hostile Indians. Troop forays out of Camp Supply, to quiet disturbances and chase roving bands of hostiles, became a daily routine. Under their new leadership the Negro troopers from Camp Supply had greater successes in the field than ever before, and their morale and confidence rose rapidly. Surely there must have been numerous settlers and others in the area, who became deeply indebted to the men of the Tenth

Cavalry for the excellent protection they provided. It was during these trying times that the Indians developed a fear of, and a healthy respect for, the colored troopers whom they named "Buffalo Soldiers." That label was an outgrowth of the fact that the Indians likened the tightly curled hair of the Negroes to the hair of buffalos. And it was during that same period that Lieutenant Colonel Davidson became known as "Black Jack Davidson." The records do not indicate the exact reasons for that title; however it probably is attributable to his association with black troops, and his coal-black hair and beard. Thus it is that Davidson was the first "Black Jack" to serve with the Tenth Cavalry. The second one came along about forty years later when "Black Jack Pershing" served with the regiment. This officer later became the famous World War I commander of the AEF, General John J. Pershing.

As the situation worsened, and hostilities became more widespread, Colonel Grierson decided to shift his headquarters from Fort Gibson back to Fort Sill. He made the move in June 1872, and stated that it would enable him to maintain a more effective control of the over-all situation. At the time of that move Davidson was flooded with the problems arising from the traders who were clustering around Camp Supply, and furnishing the Indians with liquor and firearms. He rounded up large numbers of them and had them expelled from the territory. But they merely returned to their home bases in Kansas, replenished their stocks and swarmed back into the territory. Unfortunately the military had very little legal jurisdiction over civilians, and thus were prevented from meting out appropriate punishment, other than to shoot those who resisted arrest.

Between those troublemakers and the hostile Indians, Davidson was extremely busy throughout the year 1872. In January 1873 Indian Agent Darlington complained to Davidson that five "ranches" were supplying large quantities of whiskey and firearms to the Indians. Davidson responded by sending Lieutenant Pratt, with a detachment, to arrest the ranch owners. Fifteen offenders were rounded up, and huge quantities of rot-gut whiskey, rifles, ammunition and foodstuffs were confiscated. This time the so-called peddlers were sent to Topeka, Kansas, under guard, to stand trial. They were fined $10.00 each and given one month in jail; a disgracefully low sentence for the unlawful acts they had committed. Naturally all of them rushed right back into the Oklahoma Territory as soon as they got out of jail.

Shortly after the turn of the new year, 1873, Colonel Grierson received orders to recruiting duty in the East, for a period of two or more years. As a consequence Davidson assumed command of the Tenth Cavalry and Fort Gibson on February 10, 1873. Grierson had, incidentally, moved his headquarters back to that post a few months after his move to Fort Sill. As the new commander, Davidson began a program of realigning the staff officers to effect a maximum degree of harmony while implementing his own policies. That was a customary practice whenever there was an official change in regimental commanders. Instead of an orderly transition there was strong opposition, in some quarters, to any staff changes. What actually occurred as a result of the reshuffling is somewhat blurred by conflicting accounts. Some historians have expressed the opinion that Davidson had been jealous of the loyalty of the

staff officers to Colonel Grierson. Others indicate that
Grierson was an ultra-lenient commander, especially
with the officers who were under his immediate jurisdiction. In many ways Davidson was quite the opposite.
He was a strict disciplinarian who demanded high
standards of dress, deportment, and performance from
his officers. At the same time he had a deep understanding of Negroes, their strengths, weaknesses, superstitions,
and habits. For this reason he tended to be tolerant, and
patient in his treatment of them. There is little doubt
that the staff officers resented Davidson's demands, and
were therefore not responsive to his wishes. In turn,
Davidson was not happy with the conduct of several
members of his official family, and endeavored to have
them replaced with officers of his own choosing. The
officers involved refused to comply with a request that
they resign their staff positions and return to line positions. Davidson then appealed to the adjutant-general
of the Department of Texas, in a letter dated April 10,
1873. His appeal was denied on the basis that Grierson's
assignment was only temporary, and that he would want
his own officers on the staff when he returned to the
regiment. It is interesting to note that this so-called
temporary assignment had been, from the beginning,
programmed for at least two years. From the very start,
therefore, Davidson was unpopular with several of the
regimental officers – an understandable situation since
the officers involved lost the "freedom" they enjoyed
under Grierson, and tended to look upon Davidson as
an interloper. This freedom evolved from a reason
advanced in the preceding chapter, wherein it was observed that Grierson relied unusually heavily upon his
subordinate officers for guidance, and repaid them with

an exceptionally high level of tolerance towards their unmilitary actions. Grierson's reputation as a very tolerant commander was widespread. All of this created a climate of friction in the regimental headquarters that made the command a particularly difficult task.

At this juncture the writer would like to interpose a few observations that are based upon more than thirty years of service, in ranks up to and including naval captain. There is no doubt that it was highly inappropriate for the adjutant-general to deny Davidson's request for the replacement of those officers who did not measure up to his standards. It would have been an easy matter to authorize temporary re-assignments and replacements for the two years that Grierson would be away. By his action he made the command of the Tenth Cavalry a difficult task at a time when cooperation and teamwork were highly essential. Most officers stationed in the western outposts were hard-bitten fighting men who spent a high percentage of their time in actual combat, and were hard drinkers when they relaxed. The very nature of their operations demanded loyalty to their commanders, and almost instant obedience to their orders. Such was not possible if there were friction existing between the commander and his officers. A regimental command is, in many ways, similar to that of a navy ship's captain, in that the captain's orders are a law unto themselves, and woe betide those who do not respond willingly. Under the circumstances prevailing during Davidson's tenure as commander, it could not be the commander who suffered most when his orders were disobeyed or resisted. It is a simple fact of military life that opposition to a regimental commander makes his task difficult, but causes the offender to suffer most.

The officers who were not cooperative with Davidson while he commanded the regiment, failed to take one fact into account. Davidson, who was a strict but fair commander, knew more about the art of soldiering and troop command than the whole lot of them put together, including Grierson.

History indicates that some of the recaltritant officers, in the Tenth Cavalry at that time, developed feelings of persecution. This was brought about by their own repeated acts of insubordination. It was, however, the beginning of a hate campaign that several years later resulted in some of the disgruntled officers bringing charges against Davidson. At this point it is significant to note that the relationship between Davidson and most of the officers was harmonious. The only ones with whom there were problems were the ones who were on Grierson's staff, and those company officers who were, or had been, under his immediate jurisdiction.

The enlisted men at Fort Gibson also became keenly aware of the general tightening of discipline after Davidson took command. Until then they had been allowed to gamble in the barracks, and had many other freedoms that were not usually permitted on army posts. Among the new regulations issued by Davidson was one which forbade gambling in the barracks. Typical of soldiers, however, they soon found a way around that restriction – they simply pushed up the ceiling boards in the barracks, and did their gambling in the attic.

The troubles with hostile Indians constantly worsened, and the authorities concluded that a better control could be maintained by concentrating most of the Tenth Cavalry at Fort Sill, since it was situated in the heart of the problem area. In response to orders, Davidson shifted his command to Fort Sill on April 21, 1873, and assumed command of that fort in addition to the regimental command. Fort Sill had, incidentally, been commanded by Major Schofield, Tenth Cavalry, from the time of Grierson's departure for Fort Gibson until Davidson arrived. Upon arrival at Fort Sill, Davidson expressed pleasure at the opportunity it afforded for him to become acquainted with practically all of the officers of the Tenth. Heretofore they had been scattered in small detachments in various outposts, and seldom, if ever, in the proximity of their regimental commander. As would be customary with any commander, Davidson began to look them over with a critical eye in order to size up their capabilities and efficiencies. Quite naturally this caused a feeling of uneasiness and apprehension to permeate the ranks of those officers who were strangers to Davidson. And, at the same time, there was a large scale reshuffling of quarters assignments, due to the influx of new families. A quarrel soon broke out over the reassignments to quarters, and accusations began to fly in all directions. Most of the accusations seemed to be directed at a Lieutenant Foulk and his family. It seems that they had a son who was a particular hellion, and kept things in a constant turmoil. The situation soon reached explosive proportions, forcing the post commander to take corrective action. Davidson found a neat solution to this very touchy problem. He recognized Foulk as a good officer, and succeeded in having Foulk promoted and transferred to another post. That, incidentally, is a process that later became known as "kicking him upstairs." After Foulk's transfer the atmosphere along officers' row began to clear, and harmony was eventually restored. According to the reports that filtered back to Fort Sill, the Foulk youngster continued to stir up as much trouble as ever.

During the period while the Tenth Cavalry was assembling at Fort Sill, the commanding general, Department of Texas, instigated an inspection of the regiment and of Fort Sill. Major John Hatch of the Inspector General's Department conducted the inspection. He was thorough and efficient, devoting several days to the task of looking at all phases of regimental activities. When his task was completed the resulting report highlighted the discrimination against Negro troopers, and brought the entire problem into sharp focus. In closing that phase of the report he stated,[5]

> The morale and spirit prevailing among the troopers was exceptionally high, and they are well trained and disciplined. The desertion rate is lower than any other regiment in existence.

In other areas, however, he was very critical. His paraphrased remarks are,

> Many of the mounts are cast off from the Seventh Cavalry, and others are too old for active service under combat conditions; some are ex-artillery horses that could not be retrained as cavalry mounts. F company has but forty-eight horses, with all but three of them well past fifteen years of age. In spite of all this the horses are well cared for.
>
> As for equipment, practically all of it is old, but maintained in good condition. Over thirty of the saddles in constant use were long since condemned as completely unsuited for further use.
>
> The armament situation is utterly appalling. The carbines are largely antiquated, and the ammunition supply is barely sufficient to equip each soldier with twenty rounds.

Major Hatch's report actually summarized and emphasized the many similar reports that had been made

---

[5] Old Post Records, Fort Sill Museum, Fort Sill, Okla.; and Post Returns, National Archives, Washington, D.C.

by the regimental, battalion and company commanders on numerous occasions. He concluded the report by reiterating the fact that the regiment had a good, if not spectacular, record in the field with excellent discipline, and a below average court-martial and desertion rate.

Throughout the year 1873 the Tenth Cavalry was engaged in almost constant skirmishes with large and small bands of hostile Indians who were raiding ranches, settlements and small military outposts. The Buffalo Soldiers' record of accomplishments was especially noteworthy, but for their deeds little credit came to them. Although the army knew and recognized their efforts, the news and other publicity media managed to find ways to avoid giving them the credit that was justly earned. Much of this was in a rather subtle manner, in which Negro accomplishments were given the "once-over-lightly" treatment, while the participation of white organizations was over-emphasized. It was many long years before the Buffalo Soldiers began to receive the recognition they deserved. Nevertheless, the morale of those Black soldiers remained at a high level.

About three months after Davidson's arrival at Fort Sill the Indian Agent, Mr. Tatum, was replaced with a Mr. James Haworth. Both of these men were Quakers who were generally soft, and overly trusting of the Indians under their supervision. The relationship that had existed between Davidson and Tatum was peaceful, though not cordial. With the change the climate deteriorated badly since Haworth and Davidson could not agree on much of anything pertaining to Indian management. The main reasons for this revolved around Davidson's belief in a policy of firmness in the control of the Indians on their reservation; whereas Haworth favored very soft treatment which, incidentally, is one that Grierson had always followed. Davidson simply would not agree that the reservation Indians were friendly, and firmly believed that a large-scale war with them was imminent. His beliefs seemed to be justified when, in early August, reports began filtering in from post commanders in the area, that Indian attacks were sharply increasing. These reports, coupled with the fact that he was somewhat new to the area in the vicinity of Fort Sill, caused Davidson to decide upon a scouting trip to learn about the terrain he would operate in if war did break out.

On August 15, 1873, Black Jack Davidson led four companies of the Tenth Cavalry out of Fort Sill, on a mission designed to scout the surrounding territory, make a show of force to the potentially hostile Indians, and to punish any who were off their reservations on raids into Texas. At Gilbert Creek he was joined by two additional companies of the Tenth from Fort Richardson, Texas. The expedition marched along Cache Creek to the Red River, then turned west to Buck Creek where he turned north to the Elm Fork of the Red River, and then back to Fort Sill, arriving on September 14, 1873. During the march no hostiles were encountered, but a wealth of signs indicated that they had been very active. One fresh grave was located that contained the body of a surveyor who had been murdered by the Indians. Davidson's report to the adjutant-general, Department of Texas, gave a detailed account of the mission and concluded with,[6]

Evidence was found to spare that the Indians are constantly marauding across the borders of Texas, that the reservation is a

---

[6] *Ibid.*

"City of Refuge" for them, that it is almost impossible for our troops to catch an enemy with the eye of a hawk and the stealth of a wolf, who knows every foot of the country, and that an effective method of stopping this state of affairs, while the Government feeds and clothes the reservation Indians, is to dismount them and make them account for themselves daily.

That report verified the opinions of both Generals Sherman and Sheridan, which they had expressed to the authorities in Washington on numerous occasions.

While on the scouting expedition, incidentally, an ugly rumor got started, and received a great deal of publicity in the *New York Times*. In its edition of August 29, 1873, a lengthy article stated that hostile Indians had attacked and sacked Fort Sill. Upon learning of this Davidson immediately released dispatches denying the story and demanding a retraction by the *Times*. Undoubtedly others took a hand, and exerted pressure on the newspaper. In the September 9, 1873, issue the *Times* did retract the story, and said that the whole episode was a hoax.

8

Fort Sill—Fort Griffin

While Colonel Davidson, and the main body of the Tenth Cavalry, was on the scouting mission in Western Oklahoma, in August 1873, a highly significant event occurred. An Indian Agent, Mr. Thomas Battey, a Quaker missionary, had been making strong pleas to Governor Davis, of Texas, to have Chiefs Satanta and Big Tree released from prison. He contended that the Indians in the area had lived up to their promise to maintain peaceful conditions. Actually, however, the Indians had no intention of keeping the peace; they were only marking time in order to get their chiefs out of prison. The governor sensed this, and indicated that he would not free the chiefs. When the Indians learned of this they seized Battey, and held him hostage pending the release of the chiefs. After Battey had been held for over three weeks, Governor Davis announced that he would bring Satanta and Big Tree to Fort Sill for a conference, provided the Indians refrain from hostilities and release Battey. Unfortunately trouble then arose from an entirely unexpected source. The residents along the Texas border were fearful that by setting the chiefs free a new series of uprisings would break out, and began to complain against the governor who was seeking reelection. Much to his credit, however, he did not alter his plans, and arranged for the warden of Huntsville Prison to release Satanta and Big Tree to Lieutenant Hoffman, Tenth Cavalry, for delivery to Fort Sill. The party arrived there on September 4, 1873, and the two chiefs were lodged in the guardhouse to await the arrival of all conference participants.

Governor Davis and his staff arrived at Fort Sill on October 3, 1873, as did Mr. E. P. Smith, the Commissioner of Indian Affairs in Washington. Shortly thereafter Mr. Enoch Hoag, superintendent of the Plains Indians tribes, also showed up. Since it was such an important occasion many correspondents from eastern periodicals flocked into the fort. An interesting article, written by the correspondent for *The Nation,* was published in the October 5, 1873, issue. Among other things it said,

> This is the best arranged and most complete military post I have yet seen. The barracks, officers quarters, and quartermaster buildings are built of limestone around a square parade ground. . . Hard by are a fine hospital and guardhouse. . . My conviction is that the Quakers and their policy are a bloody nuisance. Under their management this reservation has become a "City of Refuge" for the Indians that maraud and murder in Texas. The Quakers can't keep them in the reservation. Bands of them go away from the proximity of this post, that affords them protection, under the pretext of making a buffalo hunt on the plains, and turn up in Texas, where they help themselves to scalps and horses that can easily be identified by their brands when they get here. The Quakers will not let the military force them to give them up.

On October 6, 1873, the conference was called to assemble on the parade ground in front of Colonel Davidson's headquarters. A tent fly was stretched out for shading, and a table and chairs provided for the governor and other officials. The two prisoner chiefs were brought, under guard, and seated on a bench in front of the officials. Since he was suspicious of the possible

actions of the Indians, Davidson took extra precautions.
The entire garrison were held in their quarters, all officers were on hand, and one troop of cavalry stood by in
the stables with full equipment and horses saddled. The
Indians arrived in their best finery and seated themselves on the grass around the council table. Governor
Davis opened the proceedings by saying,

> I have brought back Satanta and Big Tree. You see them. They
> were prisoners of Texas and their lives were forfeited to the
> Texans, but they have been spared – we want to be at peace with
> the Kiowas and Comanches. Satanta and Big Tree can tell you
> how they were treated while prisoners in Texas.

At that point the governor was interrupted by the father
of Satanta, a very old and frail Indian, who made a
strong plea for the release of his son. He went on to
say that he wanted them to quit raiding in Texas. Satanta
then stepped forward and said he would honor his
father's wishes, and that he had been treated kindly
while in Texas. He concluded his remarks by saying,

> My heart feels big today and I will take my Texas father to my
> breast and hold him there. . . Whatever the White man
> thinks best I want my people to do. Strip off these prison clothes,
> turn me over to my people, and they will keep their promise.

The governor deliberated for a few moments, then
outlined the conditions he would require them to meet
before the two prisoners would be released. They were:
the inauguration of a revised method of drawing rations, the answering of frequent roll calls, the surrender-
ing of all their arms, and that they become farmers. His
concluding remarks were,

> In the meantime Satanta and Big Tree are to remain in the
> guardhouse until the Commanding Officer of Fort Sill is satisfied

that these conditions have been carried out. When released they must further understand that Satanta and Big Tree are liable to rearrest for their old crimes if they break these conditions, that they are not pardoned. I have consulted with Commissioner Smith and General Davidson and am satisfied that if you really desire peace you can carry out these terms. If these conditions are not complied with, it will be better for the people of Texas to resort to open war and settle this matter at once.

Indian Agent Haworth hastened to disclaim any part in the terms laid down by the governor, in an effort to convince the Indians that such conditions did not originate with him.

The assembled Indians discussed the terms for a few moments, then Lone Wolf, principal chief of the Kiowas, stepped up and made this reply to the Governor,

This is a good day. I have heard the speech of the Governor of Texas and I and my young men have taken it all up. It is the very talk I would make to these people myself.

Many more speeches were made by the several chiefs who were present, some favored the governor's conditions, and others opposed them. In general they endeavored to convince the governor that Satanta and Big Tree should be released immediately upon the promise to conform to the conditions thereafter. To all these arguments Governor Davis listened carefully, but did not alter his position. Even the Indian agents sided with the Indians. One of them, by name of Hoag, made a new attack, and in sneering tones said,

I would like to ask the Governor, does he mean to leave it discretionally with the commanding officer of the post when to release the prisoners?

The governor shot back with,

I will give it to you in writing sir. I have implicit confidence in

General Davidson. I have known him for years, and believe that when he sees the conditions fulfilled he will release them. They can comply in thirty days if they wish to.[1]

More arguments ensued, and the atmosphere, among the Indians, became supercharged with emotions. The governor remained adamant, however, and the meeting broke up for the day.

All the next day Commissioner Smith and Agent Haworth worked on the governor in an effort to convince him that his position should be changed. He did, finally, consent to one more meeting with the Indians, at which time he intimated that the prisoners would be released. The Indians remained sullen and suspicious, and left to hold a secret meeting that night. The following morning found the Indians fully prepared to kick up a big row, and they arrived at the day's meeting with arms concealed under their blankets. The governor, however, stepped out of the door of the headquarters building and made a short speech, alluding to the faithful performance of the chiefs in response to the obligations imposed by the government. Then he turned the two prisoner chiefs over to their people, without a pardon. Thus Satanta and Big Tree had the same status as a parole. They embraced the governor, and left for their camps on the prairie. In this manner the emergency was averted for the time being. Nevertheless, the Indians were unusually restless, which caused the commander of Fort Sill to be most apprehensive. He took action to insure that everything stood in readiness for instant action.

While all of that was taking place new and vigorous horses began to arrive in Fort Sill. Wagon trains were

[1] Wilbur S. Nye, *Carbine and Lance: The Story of Old Fort Sill.*

also rolling in almost daily, with late model carbines, new revolvers, and ample quantities of ammunition. That raised the morale of the troopers to new highs, especially when they began to realize how much their effectiveness had been increased. This manifested itself each time a patrol in the field encountered any of the bands of hostile Indians that were constantly roaming, and raiding off of their reservations.

The reports brought back by these patrols made Davidson keenly aware of the fact that his apprehensions were well founded. It was becoming increasingly evident that the Quaker Indian agents were wholly ineffective in maintaining peaceful conditions among their charges. In fact, the Quakers seemed to be indifferent to the need for protecting the settlers in the area, in spite of their frequent experiences with the treacherous elements of the various tribes. Instead of asking the military to maintain discipline among the Indians, they endeavored to prevent it from so doing. In the process there was a great deal of unfairness towards those Indians who had been faithful to their obligations to the government, in that the warring Indians received the same protection as those who were innocent. The resulting situation was that the hostiles actually did use their reservations as sanctuaries, and ranged far afield to raid settlements in Texas. An ironic situation arose in one raid when the Indians stole all of the stock belonging to the Indian Agent Haworth. But even that did not cause him to lose faith in the Indians.

Time after time Black Jack requested authority to take to the field in order to chase down and punish the guilty Indians, but was unable to get the necessary approval. The lack of punitive military action encouraged the hostiles to become more bold than ever before. The Cheyennes, for example, sent word through an emissary that they were going to clean out Fort Sill, and kill all of its inhabitants. The locally situated Indians, upon learning of the threat, decided to beat the distantly-located Cheyennes to the punch. They began to raid teamsters who were bringing supplies to the fort, men who were cutting wood for contractors, and even whites who were friendly to them. A great many murders were committed. On July 13, 1874, the Indians attacked a camp about eleven miles from Fort Sill, ran off with fifty head of cattle, and murdered one of the herders. Davidson then dispatched a lieutenant with a detachment of troopers to investigate. Upon his return the lieutenant reported the circumstances to Davidson, which prompted him to issue this order,

> Fort Sill, July 17, 1874. – The hostile bands of Comanches, Cheyennes, and Kiowas having committed depredations and murders upon Government employees within the reservation, and within a few miles of this post, some marked line must be drawn between the hostile and friendly portions of those tribes. In order that the troops and others may be able to distinguish those who are friendly – all such Indians must form their camps on the east of Cache Creek at points selected by the Agent.[2]

Under the circumstances that order certainly was not out of line. Nevertheless, Indian Agent Haworth became very angry and protested the order. His main reason was stated to be that there was no grazing for stock on the east bank of Cache Creek. His statement was correct since the grass had been burned off by Chief Lone Wolf a few days earlier when he started a prairie fire to hide his movements. Colonel Davidson paid no

---

[2] Old Post Records, Fort Sill Museum.

attention to Haworth. In fact, he issued a follow-up order which would permit, "No Indian to enter the post unless accompanied by the interpreter, Mr. Jones."

News of these highly critical conditions reached General Sherman who immediately suggested to General Sheridan that he add more cavalry units to those concentrated at Fort Sill, in order to insure the safety of the post. That was done without delay. Sherman then requested and received permission from the President to have all Indians enrolled, by name, and to consider those who refused to comply as hostiles. In addition the army was directed to round up the hostiles, punish them, and force their return to the reservations where they could be treated as prisoners of war.

That order, and a directive for the army to assume the management of hostile Indians, was received simultaneously by Colonel Davidson and the Indian agent, on July 26, 1874. On the following day Davidson published an order which required all friendly Indians to enroll by August 3. Indian Agent Haworth was absolutely furious, and protested the short time allowed for the enrollment. Davidson replied that the time was deliberately made brief in order to prevent the influx of the entire group of hostile Comanches, who might intimidate the friendlies and thus prevent their enrollment. Haworth again tried to delay the enrollment by saying that it would take him at least one month to complete the task. Black Jack snapped back that he could easily complete the job in two days. Haworth lapsed into sullen silence and refused to have anything to do with the enrollment. Davidson ignored him, and detailed certain of his officers to perform the task of enrolling the Indians in the general proximity of the fort. For those further afield Davidson left Fort Sill on July 30 with three companies of cavalry, to visit Indian camps and make the enrollment. The job was completed without incident on August 13, 1874. However, he noted an abundance of signs which indicated that many bands of hostiles lurked in the countryside. It seemed evident from these signs that hostilities would soon break out.

On August 21, 1874, at six o'clock in the evening, Black Jack Davidson was sitting on the veranda of his quarters, in shirt sleeves, sipping a cooling drink, when an orderly rode up and handed him a message. It was an urgent dispatch from Captain Lawson, who commanded a company of infantry guarding the Wichita Agency, which stated that a band of Comanches, under Chief Red Food, was camped at the agency and acting hostile. Davidson immediately ordered four troops of the Tenth Cavalry to prepare to march with full arms, and good mounts. They left Fort Sill at ten o'clock that same evening, with Black Jack riding at the head of the column, and headed for Anadarko, some thirty-seven miles south. The following day was the regularly designated day for issuing rations to the various tribes in the vicinity of Anadarko. Beef was issued to the friendly Indians in the morning, and they began to butcher the steers immediately. Red Food's Comanches were on hand to help themselves to the meat as fast as it was dressed, by raiding the friendlies. At about ten in the morning information reached Anadarko that Davidson's column was rapidly approaching, and everything quieted down for the time being. Davidson arrived about noon and sent for Red Food. When the Chief arrived he was informed, by Davidson, that he and his people must give themselves up as prisoners of war, and surrender their weapons.

Davidson detailed a lieutenant and forty men to accompany Red Food to his camp, to receive the surrender of the warriors. They refused to give up their bows and arrows, on the basis that it had never before been required. The lieutenant sent a messenger back to get the colonel's decision. While waiting for the messenger to return, some Kiowas, on the outskirts of the camp, began to taunt the Comanches. Red Food, who had an especially short fuse, leaped from his horse and waved a blanket to frighten the other horses, then ran into the brush. The soldiers fired at him with little effect, but that started a brisk fight. The yelling and shouting of the Indians created a terrific racket. Davidson, who was approaching at a trot, heard the noise and led his detachment at full gallop to the scene of the rumpus. The Indians took to their heels with troopers in hot pursuit. At the same time Captain Lawson, and his infantrymen, were busily engaged in clearing the area of other hostiles.

When the area became reasonably quiet Davidson ordered his entire command to advance upon the camp of the hostiles. The cavalry troopers were thus lined up with their backs to the commissary and, as they moved forward, some of the hostiles who had been lurking behind various buildings began to fire upon the troopers. Two cavalrymen and several horses were wounded, and the situation became extremely awkward. If the troopers opened fire there was great danger of having friendly Indians in their line of fire. Instead, therefore, they took after the hostiles who were heading for the nearby woods, apparently with the intention of scattering and attacking from all sides. When the troopers reached the woods they again dismounted and followed the Indians into the woods, but the Indians just faded away. Davidson ordered his force to remount and give chase across the nearby river. Employing a series of hit-and-run tactics the Indians eluded the troopers, and kept the entire area in a turmoil all through the night. At daylight Davidson organized his forces into one large group to defend the Wichita Agency, and several smaller groups to fan out and chase the various bands of hostiles. In this manner a semblance of order was restored, the friendly Indians were sorted out from the hostiles, and the agency was saved. In the process it was learned that some of the hostiles were a tribe of Kiowas who had been professing friendship. The hard-fought battle ended in a highly satisfactory manner.

While that battle was in progress the somewhat-doubtful Indians began to realize that the government forces were in earnest about promises that were made, and had the strength to enforce compliance. In excess of three hundred hostiles had engaged in the uprising, and they suffered heavy losses. The only losses to the army were four troopers wounded, none seriously. The uprising became known as the "Battle of the Anadarko." It was the direct cause of the surrender, a short time later, of about 479 Comanches, 585 Kiowas, and 306 Kiowa-Apache hostiles. However, it was a well-known fact that far greater numbers of hostiles fled to their favorite haunts west of the mountains. Those haunts were situated in an area between the Canadian River on the north, and the Brazos River on the south, which was very rough country with poor and inadequate water, and insufficient grass for grazing animals. That area had never been explored in detail, and was too poorly mapped to permit the movement of large bodies of troops. Consequently, the hostiles enjoyed relative immunity.[3]

Although fully cognizant of the difficulties involved, General Sheridan was preparing plans to converge on that area from all four sides. He planned to have Colonel Nelson A. Miles move in from the north, Colonel Ranald Mackenzie to come up from the south, Majors Price and Buell to move from the west, and Black Jack Davidson to advance from the east. When issued the plan directed all units to be in full force, and to keep the Indians constantly on the move until their will to resist had been weakened. It was the general's hope that this plan would be the most humane, and that it would make the Indians surrender without causing too much bloodshed. Sheridan endeavored to develop his plans with the utmost care, because of the extreme bitterness against the army that existed among the Cheyennes and some of the other tribes who camped in those hills. That bitterness was the outgrowth of Custer's massacre of Black Kettle's sleeping village, on November 27, 1868. As was mentioned earlier, Black Kettle was then well-known as the "Peace Chief." Custer's attack occurred in the general vicinity of the town later named Cheyenne, Oklahoma. That area was included in the sweep planned by General Sheridan.

At Fort Sill preparations for the activation of Sheridan's plan moved ahead at a fast pace, and were completed by the first of September, 1874. On September 10, Davidson led a force of six companies of Tenth Cavalry, three companies of infantry, and a section of

---

[3] Nye, *Carbine and Lance.*

mountain howitzers out of Fort Sill. Before leaving he arranged for adequately protecting the fort, during his absence, by leaving two companies of cavalry and two of infantry in the fort. He also provided for guarding the Wichita Agency, where the outbreak occurred the previous month, by stationing three companies of infantry there, under the command of Captain Lawson.

As directed in the attack plan, Davidson led his force in the direction of the area known as the "Staked Plains," in the Texas Panhandle, west of Fort Sill. Constant skirmishes occurred with marauding bands of Indians, which succeeded in slowing his advance. In each of these engagements punishment was meted out by the well-prepared soldiers from Fort Sill. On October 24 Davidson accepted the surrender of a large band of Comanches on Elk Creek. He then pushed northward toward Sweetwater, in bitterly cold weather, during which twenty-four troopers were disabled by severe cases of frostbite. Adding to the difficulties was the loss of more than one hundred animals when they froze to death. Supplies were running low, with little chance for replenishment due to the inability of heavy supply wagons to get through the heavy snowfall. By early November the weather began to clear somewhat, and they made a little better progress. On November 6, Major Price, with a patrol from the Eighth Cavalry, ran into a group of more than one hundred hostiles. He immediately called for help. Davidson, who was not far away, sent two companies of the Tenth Cavalry to assist. The hostiles were overtaken on November 8, soundly thrashed, and forced to retreat in haste.

Davidson continued moving toward the North Fork of the Red River, reaching the broken country near the head of the North Fork, where it cuts into the edge of the Staked Plains. Here they found the mutilated body of a trooper, and paused long enough to give him a decent burial. The hostiles continued fleeing to the north where they were sighted by Colonel Miles, but his horses were too exhausted to pursue them. Miles called upon Davidson for assistance, and he responded by dispatching Captain Viele with one hundred picked men. Viele followed the Indians, overtaking rear guards, abandoned property and many horses. But the main body of hostiles faded into the Llano Estacado wasteland, an area so large that they could only be found by accident. Viele turned back when he reached Muster Creek, and rejoined Davidson's column as it moved slowly toward McClellan Creek. When Davidson reached that creek he turned north to the Sweetwater, which was the farthest point he reached during the campaign. The area he was now moving through was especially bad, being extremely rugged, full of sand dunes, shin oak, gullies, and most of the water was alkaline. There was no supply base for the troops, and grazing for the animals was practically non-existent. Adding to their difficulties was the lack of extra mounts, and when the horses tired the troopers had to dismount and walk. By November 18, all forage was exhausted, food supplies were at a dangerously low level, and the supply wagons from Fort Sill, more than two hundred miles distant, had not arrived. On that day a fierce storm roared in from the north, dropping the temperature far below zero in less than two hours. Several animals died of cold and hunger, and many men suffered frostbite.

While the column moved slowly in the direction of Fort Sill, Captain Viele made a detailed report of the results of his chase, stating that he had pursued the hostiles until they had been dispersed, and lost most of their stock. As a consequence of Viele's relentless chase the Cheyennes attempted to escape across the Staked Plains into New Mexico. They lived to regret that attempt because of their unfamiliarity with that territory, and the lack of buffalo for food. Other Indians began moving to the east, in the direction of the agencies and reservations. Davidson continued moving eastward with extreme difficulty, over ground that was completely covered with ice. Progress continued to be slow as the force marched down the North Fork of the Red River, to the vicinity of Gypsum Bluffs. At that point they were met by Captain Lawson with a wagon train loaded with forage and other much needed supplies. The troops refreshed themselves with hot food, and donned fresh, warm clothing. They did not pause for long. The march continued eastward to Elk Creek and then south to Fort Sill, where they arrived on November 29, 1874. The Indian troubles were not over, however, for information was delivered to Davidson, immediately after his arrival, that a serious uprising had occurred a few miles northwest of Fort Sill. He sent Captain Keyes, and a detachment of fifty troopers, to restore order. The captain returned several days later with more than fifty warriors whom he had taken prisoners.

The incident settled by Captain Keyes brought the war to an end. It was officially designated the "Red River War," and acclaimed to be an outstandingly successful endeavor. The statistical record of accomplishments during that campaign proves that the forces led by Black Jack Davidson compiled an enviable record. That force, alone, scouted more miles, destroyed more

Indian property and equipment, captured more prisoners (over four hundred), and rounded up over two
thousand of the Indians' animals. In all this he had not
lost a single man. Of course, the other forces, led by
Mackenzie, Miles, Price and Buell are deserving of
great praise also, because their accomplishments were
noteworthy indeed. As a result of that war, the pacifica-
tion of this plains area was achieved for the time being.
Of that campaign General Sheridan, in his report to
General Sherman, stated,

> This campaign was not only comprehensive, but was the most
> successful of any Indian Campaign in this country since its settle-
> ment by the whites; and much credit is due to the officers and
> men engaged in it. . . The high standard of honor and in-
> tegrity attained by the officers and men is deserving of commen-
> dation. . . The result of my observations makes me believe
> the moral standing of the officers and men in the service is higher
> at the present time than at any period within my knowledge.

That statement by General Sheridan, together with his
complete report of the Red River War, formed a part of
the Secretary of War's annual report for the year 1875.[4]

During the month of December 1874, Davidson resolved to try persuasion with the Indians, instead of
force. However, since he believed the Cheyennes could
not be trusted, he stripped them of their guns as they
surrendered, and had them held under close guard.
With some of the other tribes his policy of persuasion
was aided by Chief Kicking Bird, who induced the particularly rebellious Chief Big Bow to give himself up
in exchange for immunity instead of punishment. That
turned out to be an excellent bargain, in that Big Bow,

---

[4] Information on the Red River War is drawn from this Annual Report,
and from Old Post Records, Fort Sill Museum, Nye, *Carbine and Lance,* and
other books on the subject.

in turn, brought in five additional chiefs with more than two hundred warriors, and four hundred head of their stock. Colonel Davidson gave a full accounting of that series of events in his report to General Augur (number 3490-1874) dated December 23, 1874.

Davidson issued general orders to all activities in the vicinity of Fort Sill spelling out his revised policies in detail for their guidance. For the next few weeks the results being experienced gave every indication that the newly established policies were highly successful. Only one incident arose to mar what promised to be a completely peaceful situation. An uprising by a roving band of Kiowas caused Davidson to lead a striking force to run them down. On the Salt Fork of the Red River, in Texas, he overtook the fleeing Indians and captured sixty-five warriors, one hundred and seventy-five women and children, three hundred ponies and seventy mules. Among those captured were Chiefs Lone Wolf, Red Otter and Lean Bull. After that everything became exceedingly quiet in the general vicinity of Fort Sill.

Unfortunately, Davidson was not permitted to remain at Fort Sill to enjoy the fruits of the new policies of Indian management. The over-all army policy of periodically rotating regiments between different posts caused a change to occur for the Tenth Cavalry. On March 27, 1875, all of the Tenth Cavalry personnel then stationed at Fort Sill, were transferred to Fort Griffin, Texas, with Davidson assigned to command the post. The new occupants of Fort Sill were the Fourth Cavalry and its commander, Colonel R. S. Mackenzie. The incoming commander liked what he found, and continued with great success the Indian policies that had been established by Davidson.

Within a few weeks after the change to Fort Griffin, Colonel Grierson returned to resume command of the Tenth Cavalry. He established his headquarters, and moved the staff personnel to join him at Fort Concho, in western Texas. At that time about one-third of Davidson's Tenth Cavalry troops were also relocated to Fort Concho. As would be expected, the staff officers were delighted to get away from Davidson, and return to Grierson. At the same time Davidson experienced a great feeling of relief when those troublesome officers left his jurisdiction. Davidson remained in command of Fort Griffin.

As a result of their change in location, the main thrust of the Tenth Cavalry's mission in the Fort Griffin area was altered somewhat. While stationed in the Oklahoma Territory they had been primarily concerned with the control of hostile Indians. Their collateral duty was to furnish protection to the great cattle drives that passed over the Chisolm Trail, several miles west of Fort Sill. In the Fort Griffin area the Indian menace had abated considerably, but the cattle drives were imperiled as much as ever, and probably more. Through Texas swarms of rustlers and outlaws preyed on these drives, using modern weapons, and operating in well-organized gangs. The Chisholm Trail, the heaviest traveled of the several trails, passed between Forts Griffin and Richardson to the east, and was constantly harassed by these outlaws. As a consequence, at least two troops of the Tenth Cavalry were in the field at all times, patrolling the trails. They would remain on station for three to four weeks, ranging as much as three hundred miles north and south, and covering wide areas on each side of the trail. Constant efforts were made to flush out the marauding bands of outlaws. Although their protection of the drovers was generally effective, a few of the raiders managed to break through to prey upon the trail herds. Nevertheless, the cattle drovers fully understood the magnitude of the task faced by the cavalrymen, which would often be complicated by the appearance of hostile bands of Indians. It is certain that the cattlemen had a healthy respect for their Black protectors.

The magnitude of the task of protecting the cattle drives, during the 1870s, is best visualized by noting the large numbers of cattle passing over the trails. The drives originated in the general vicinity of San Antonio, Texas, and moved north to the railroad shipping points in Kansas at Wichita, Dodge City, Ellsworth and Ellis. The annual number of cattle moving along the trails varied from a low of two hundred one thousand, to more than seven hundred thousand. Both Forts Griffin and Richardson were headquarters for providing the troops to protect the trails.

After Davidson arrived in Fort Griffin he began to suffer from recurrent attacks of malaria. Although he had experienced a few minor attacks while in Fort Sill, they were nothing to compare with the ones that struck him after the move to Texas. On more than one occasion they forced him into bed for days at a time. Since he once had been denied the opportunity of a physical retirement, there seemed to be no opportunity for another hearing before a retiring board. Therefore, he determined to carry on at all costs. That decision almost cost him his life one time, when his temperature rose to a critically high level. When that occurred the post surgeon prevailed upon him to request a leave of absence, in order to regain his health in a more favorable climate.

He followed that advice, and was granted a four-month leave of absence. The entire Davidson family then moved back to the family home in Manhattan, Kansas. Upon his arrival there early in August of 1875, Davidson placed himself in the hands of a civilian doctor. It was fortunate that he did so, because during the rest of that summer he suffered one relapse after another.

When the four-month period of leave neared its end, his physical condition indicated that a return to duty was improbable in the near future. He therefore submitted a "Certificate for Absence on Account of Sickness" to the departmental commander, which stated, in part,

> I am suffering from Chronic Diarrhea with derangement of the stomach and liver caused by malarial poisoning at Forts Sill and Griffin – also with kidneys badly affected, with symptoms of Diabetes, and that I am now under a physicians treatment and have been for over two months, since 17th July '75, and that in consequence thereof I am, in my opinion, unfit for duty, and not able to resume my duties in a less period than thirty days.

At the same time he wrote a personal letter to his old friend, General Sherman, who was then Commander U.S. Army, outlining his problem. In reply Sherman wrote as follows,[5]

Headquarters Army of the United States
Genl. J. W. Davidson   St. Louis, Mo., Aug. 30, 1875
Manhattan, Kansas
Dear Davidson: Your friendly letter of Aug. 26 is received and I hasten to assure you that you may depend on me for an extension of your leave. It is in the aggregate not to exceed four months, the limit authorized by the War Dept. as within my power – but I understand yours is a sick leave which you can prolong monthly by obtaining the usual Medical Certificate.

---

[5] Original of this letter is in the author's file.

St. Louis, Mo. Aug 30 1875

Genl J. W. Davidson
  Manhattan Kansas
Dear Davidson

  Your friendly letter of Aug 26. is received and I hasten to assure you that you may depend on me for an extension of your leave. It is in the opposite policy not to exceed four months; the limit settled by the War Dept. is within my power — but I understand yours is a sick leave, which you can prolong monthly by obtaining the usual Medical Certificate.

  I think you are wise in now providing a home for your family — for army life at all times most precarious, seems to me peculiarly so at this time. I advise you to take advantage of the extremely low price of land at this time to secure enough close to your parental home, to make up a small farm. I know several retired officers who have thus made comfortable provision for their families.

  I saw Mr McGunigle a few days ago. and he looked as hearty & healthy as he did thirty years ago. I hope you and Mrs Davidson are in comparatively good health and if the sympathy of a large circle of friends is the source of comfort you certainly possess it.

  In my recent trips I met hundreds of officers all of whom spoke of the sad affliction which had overtaken your family. Remember me kindly to Mrs Davidson and your family,

  Truly your friend
    W. T. Sherman
      General —

GENERAL WILLIAM T. SHERMAN'S LETTER TO DAVIDSON

SHERMAN HOUSE, THE POST COMMANDER'S QUARTERS AT FORT SILL

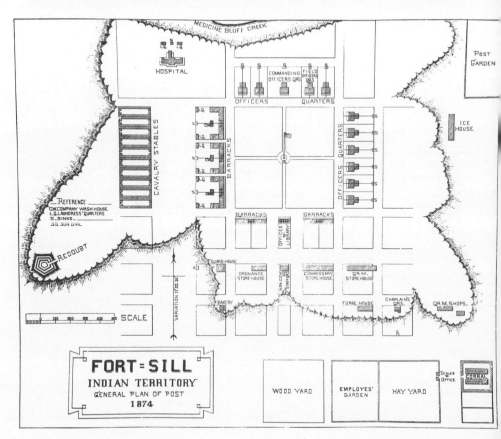

THE POST TRADER'S STORE AT FORT SILL, 1870
Tenth Cavalry Black troopers and civilians standing in front.

A FREDERIC REMINGTON SKETCH OF TENTH CAVALRY BUFFALO SOLDIERS

COMMANDER'S OFFICE, OLD POST

FROM THIS ROOM A HOST OF FAMOUS CAVALRYMEN RODE FORTH ON MISSIONS OF WAR AND PEACE IN INDIAN TERRITORY DAYS, AMONG THEM SUCH DISTINGUISHED GENERALS AS GRIERSON, SCHOFIELD, DAVIDSON, CARLTON, MACKENZIE, HATCH, MIZNER, HENRY, BENTEEN, AND SCOTT. IN 1911 AND 1912 THIS OFFICE WAS OCCUPIED BY COLONEL DAN T. MOORE, FOUNDER AND FIRST COMMANDANT OF THE FIELD ARTILLERY SCHOOL.

OLD POST HEADQUARTERS

BUILT 1870. USED AS POST HQ TO 1911. AT COUNCIL HELD HERE OCTOBER 1873 GOVERNOR DAVIS OF TEXAS FREED KIOWA CHIEFS SATANTA AND BIG TREE. 29,000 HOMESTEADERS REGISTERED HERE FOR THE OPENING OF THE TERRITORY JULY 1901. THE SCHOOL OF FIRE OCCUPIED THIS BUILDING 1911-12 AND THE SCHOOL OF MUSKETRY 1913-18.

BUILDING MARKERS AT THE OLD POST, FORT SILL

I think you are wise in now providing a home for your family – for Army life, at all times most precarious, seems to me peculiarly so at this time. I advise you to take advantage of the extremely low prices of land at this time to secure enough close to your present house to make up a small farm. I know several retired officers who have thus made comfortable provision for their families. . . Truly your Friend

W. T. SHERMAN, General

Regularly each month, following receipt of Sherman's letter, Davidson submitted a "Certificate on Account of Sickness," until a fair measure of his strength had been recovered. He so reported and received orders, on May 3, 1876, to report for duty as recruiting officer at Louisville, Kentucky. The hot and humid climate of that locality caused the same old malarial condition to reappear, almost immediately. He was, therefore, forced to return to his home on account of sickness on June 6, 1876. He soon received a six-month leave of absence, as a result of the following,

Lieut. Col. J. W. Davidson, 10th U.S. Cavalry, having applied for a certificate on which to ground an application for a leave of absence, I do hereby certify that I have examined this officer and find that he is suffering from chronic Diarrhoea, the result of frequent attacks of malarial fever, induced by exposure in the line of duty in Texas, Virginia and the Indian Territory, and that in consequence thereof, he is, in my opinion, unfit for duty. I further declare my belief that he will not be able to resume his duties in a less period than six months, and that a change beyond the limits of this Department is necessary to save his life or prevent permanent disability.

Dated at Louisville, Kentucky   ELY McCLELLAN
this 22nd day of May 1876   Asst. Surgeon, U.S. Army

Davidson had forwarded that surgeon's certificate to the adjutant-general of the army, with this letter, dated May 22, 1876,

General E. D. Townsend

General: I respectfully make application for six months leave
of absence, based upon the accompanying Certificate of Asst.
Surgeon McClellan USA.

I hoped that I could perform some duty away from the malarial posts of Texas, but I find the extreme heat here and malarial
influences also affect me as if I were in Texas.

I request this letter may be shown the General of the Army
whose kindness sent me here, and trust that the summer months
spent in the plains of Kansas and Colorado may restore my health
in a sufficient degree to return to duty in the winter months. I feel
very keenly my disability, and that is the motive of this extended
letter.

From the day the foregoing letter was dispatched to
the adjutant-general, Davidson made repeated attempts
to obtain a change in the locale of his active duty assignments. He was firmly convinced that the climatic conditions in the Southwest would continue to be detrimental
to his health. The experience of his attempt to perform
duty in Kentucky made it all the more apparent that a
return to the Tenth Cavalry in the Southwest would be
fatal. In spite of his best efforts the army authorities
seemed to ignore the whole thing, and met his requests
with stony silence. It would appear that the bureaucratic
attitude of some of the high level generals in Washington was that officers in field organizations should carry
on until they collapsed. All very fine theory for those
who were comfortably established behind desks in army
headquarters. Physical retirement appeared to Davidson to be a rare privilege, as exhibited in the retirement
proceedings of 1870. Bending, therefore, to the indif-
ference of his superiors, Davidson gritted his teeth, and
resolved to keep going until he dropped from his saddle.

9

Oklahoma
and Brewing Troubles

At the end of one year of sick leave Davidson's health returned to normal. He so reported and immediately received orders to return to the Tenth Cavalry, and to command Fort Richardson, Texas. He arrived at the new post on December 20, 1876. At that time the garrison housed four companies of the Tenth, four companies of infantry, and some artillery. The scope of this command was broadened considerably by the orders issued to Davidson. In addition to the fort, he was directed to command the District of the Upper Brazos and Fort Griffin. Griffin, located about one hundred miles to the southwest, was then commanded by Captain P. L. Lee, Tenth Cavalry, and the garrison consisted of two companies of the Tenth Cavalry.

Davidson's responsibilities included patrolling the two cattle trails which passed through the District. They were the Chisholm and Western trails. In this respect he directed the operations of the troops at Fort Griffin as well as those in Fort Richardson. This command was far more extensive than any of Davidson's former posts, as it was one of the most important commands in the Southwest. Richardson had been commanded for years by Colonel Ranald S. Mackenzie until he replaced Davidson at Fort Sill in early 1875.

Patrolling the cattle trails was, to a large extent, a summer-time operation, which began in early June and continued until late fall. During the cattle drive months the activities at Fort Richardson were exceedingly brisk. The importance of protection for the drives was discussed in the preceding chapter. That activity coupled with the discovery of coal and some minerals around the nearby town of Jacksboro, Texas, caused quite a boom. The town grew to a bustling 2,500 population, and the local newspaper often called for more settlers to move in. That paper, the *Frontier Echo,* would run news items similar to this,

> Come on gentlemen, bring your families, buy stock, subscribe for the paper, and grow in wealth and righteousness.

Since the fort was so important it had been especially well equipped with quarters. Each house for the officers had four rooms, and the one for the commander had five. However, the place had its drawbacks too. It was situated in an unhealthy spot on low ground at the confluence of two streams. Summer temperatures often ran as high as 104 degrees in the shade, then dropped as low as zero in mid-winter. It is well described in this quotation from the medical history of the fort,

> Diseases at the Post were of the unusual variety, but malaria was very common. Some contracted it in river bottoms where scouting parties camped to be near water. Most, however, originated in or near the post, since the whole area was heavily infested with mosquitos. Also dysentery was very frequent and severe. Malaria bouts often lasted for three weeks, during which body temperatures reached dangerously high levels.

The post drinking water came from a nearby spring which provided an ample supply of cool, clear water.

Although very busy, nothing of significance occurred

during the first half of 1877. Then, in June, Davidson made an inspection trip to Fort Griffin, which precipitated difficulties that arose about one year later. It seems that the post commander, Captain Lee, believed that Davidson's criticism of his method of operating the post were unnecessarily harsh. This will be covered later in this chapter.

It is especially interesting to take note of several news items that were published in the Jacksboro newspaper, the *Frontier Echo*. The first was:

[June 15, 1877] Gen. Davidson now has an evening gun fired at sunset, a ceremony that previous post commanders have honored more in the breach than in observance.

[June 22] It sounds warlike to hear the morning and evening gun at Fort Richardson. Gen. Davidson has procured a flagstaff, which will soon be erected, and then the Nation's colors will float in the breeze.

[June 29] A flagstaff has at length been planted at Fort Richardson, and the flag can now be seen flying in the breeze from sunrise to sunset. As the traveler approaches Jacksboro from the south or east he can, when miles distant, observe the flag as the first object that attracts his attention. Fort Richardson was established about 11 years ago, and has had several commanders, but to Gen. Davidson, the present one, belongs the credit, the honor of unfurling the National Emblem at that place. Long may it wave.

It is almost unbelievable that an army post, on the great plains during those troublesome years, had functioned for eleven years without observing the age-old ritual of flying the flag during daylight hours. This newspaper article would appear to verify the neglect.

In August 1877 a dispute arose, between the editor of the *Echo* and Davidson, that nearly reached serious proportions. All the details of the circumstance are not readily available, but it appears to have originated when Captain T. A. Baldwin passed erroneous information to the newspaperman. It also appears that Baldwin developed a strong feeling of antagonism toward Davidson when the latter assumed command of the fort. For a time prior to Davidson's arrival Baldwin had been in temporary command of the post, and resented the loss of prestige when he relinquished that command. The quarrel broke into the open when the following article appeared in the August 17, 1877, edition of the *Frontier Echo,*

> We learn that a superannuated old dotard started out a few days ago with the avowed intention of giving the editor of the Echo a damned good licking. As he failed to put in an appearance to date, we suppose he saw the error of his way before arriving at our den, or it may be on account of the extreme hot weather and scarcity of ice, that he concluded to forego the pleasure. The cause of his ire we do not know, but guess it to be an article which appeared in these columns a few weeks ago which, by prodigious perversion, he construes into a personal attack. If he felt aggrieved and was possessed of the instincts of a gentleman, he would first ascertain from us whether or not an insult was intended. We meant every word of it, and have none of it to take back, nor apology to offer. If he had asked us the question, we could have truthfully informed him that he was not in our thoughts when we wrote the article referred to, nor were we aware our little shaft had penetrated his manly (?) bosom until apprised of it by his howling.

There are different versions of the events which followed the publication of that article. Nevertheless, some very harsh words must have passed between the two principals. It is said, truthfully or otherwise, that Davidson finally challenged the editor of the *Frontier Echo,* Mr. George Robson, to a duel. Fortunately for every one concerned the following article appeared in the August 24 edition of the paper, which poured oil on the troubled waters,

> In an article headed, Plain talk, in last week's issue of the Echo, in the heat of passion, we used some very strong language and called a certain individual a very hard name. We worked off the paper and our anger at the same time, and expressed ourselves as sorry we applied a certain epithet to the gentleman named, and expressed our willingness to retract it; this when the paper was about half out of the press, and not one copy had gone out of the office or been read by anyone, except ourselves and compositor.
>
> The gentleman referred to called on us and asked if he was the person alluded to. We replied, that he was if he made threats against us as stated in the article referred to. He informed us that he *did not* make such a threat, and that our informant uttered a falsehood when he told us so.
>
> Taking our informant to be a gentleman, we believed him. We are now satisfied he was greatly mistaken, or wilfully stated to us that which is not so. Therefore we are satisfied we done an injustice to the gentleman reflected on, and cheerfully recall all harsh and improper words used in said article.

Within a few days General Davidson and Mr. Robson had an amiable meeting over a glass of beer, and completely cleared the air. During that meeting Mr. Robson stated that Captain Baldwin gave him the erroneous information that precipitated the affair. The action taken against Baldwin by Davidson is not clearly indicated in the records, but it is significant to note that Baldwin, and his company, were ordered to Fort Concho, Texas, a short time later. At that time Colonel Grierson commanded Fort Concho. The story of the Davidson-Robson dispute became somewhat clearer when, on February 4, 1878, Mr. Robson wrote a statement which detailed the episode, from his point of view. He definitely does implicate Baldwin as the one who made the erroneous statements about Davidson's threats.

One copy of that statement was given to Captain Baldwin and the other to Davidson, and the Davidson copy is in the files of this writer.

Late in September 1877, a directive to the post commander instructed Davidson to make preparations for closing Fort Richardson. That was prompted by the fact that cattle drive activities were steadily decreasing on the Chisholm Trail, and moving to the west. That caused the army patrols from Richardson to travel long distances before reaching their operating areas. And, of course, Indian and outlaw activities moved with the trail herds. On January 19, 1878, Davidson and most of the troops under his command moved to Fort Sill, leaving a small caretaker force behind. Fort Richardson closed forever on May 23, 1878.

Upon arrival at Fort Sill, with four companies of the Tenth Cavalry, Davidson relieved Colonel Mackenzie of the post command. Mackenzie then left with most of the Fourth Cavalry for a new post to the north. That change was made at a time when the Indian hostilities in the Fort Sill area were increasing rapidly. Since Davidson's force was considerably smaller than Mackenzie's, it needed to be strengthened. Additional troops were, therefore, sent from Forts Concho and Griffin. They were three companies of the Tenth Cavalry, Companies A, G, and I, commanded by Captains Nolan, Lee and Baldwin respectively. Baldwin and Lee were especially unhappy over the move, since both held grudges against Davidson.

The influx of the three companies caused a large scale reshuffling of married-officers' assignments. That occurred at a time when the existing occupants had barely settled in after their move from Richardson. As always occurred in such cases, the wives began to bicker among themselves, and to heckle their husbands to get quarters more to their liking. This put Davidson in an awkward position since he was bound by army regulations, which required that officers' quarters be assigned according to the rank and seniority of those concerned. Having followed those rules, Davidson was virtually powerless to accommodate anyone. What started as a tempest in a teapot soon reached explosive proportions, and strong measures were necessary in order to control the situation. Davidson, therefore, tightened the discipline of the command, primarily that of the officers. What preceded the issuance of official reprimands does not appear in the records. Whatever it was must have been ineffective, because a number of officers received them. They were issued for such infractions as sloppy dress, unmilitary bearing, failure to salute properly, and absence from reveille or retreat roll calls. Of all those taken to task only three were repeat offenders. They were: Nolan two, Lee three, and Baldwin seven or more.[1]

It is interesting to take note of the fact that, of all the twenty-five plus officers on the post, including cavalry, infantry and artillery, none had any great difficulty in complying with the stricter discipline except Baldwin, Lee and Nolan. What made bad matters worse is that those three were company commanders, who were obligated to set examples for their juniors. After the second reprimand Captain Nolan seemed to fall in line, but Baldwin and Lee began to bicker with the post commander. Some time later these "malcontents" claimed that Davidson started the quarrel by threatening to have

---

[1] Information about the official reprimands was gleaned from the old post records, Fort Sill Museum.

them "black booked," an action that could be detrimental to their future promotional prospects. Their
reasoning was to the effect that Davidson had been in
the wrong by demanding such high disciplinary standards of the officers.

Based upon a reading of much that has been recorded
by historical writers, and comparing that with Davidson's personal file, the conclusion is drawn that a onesided picture of Black Jack Davidson has been painted.
Since both Captains Baldwin and Lee hated him with
a passion, they headed a "Let's get Davidson society."
Everything pertaining to the origin of that hate may
never be known, but we can consider a few facts that
have not heretofore been published. Baldwin and Davidson met for the first time when the latter assumed
command of Fort Richardson, and Baldwin took offense
at losing the post command. Captain Lee's hatred evidently stems from Davidson's inspection of Fort Griffin
in 1877. That inspection was necessary because one of
the garrisoned soldiers had been murdered. From it
Davidson gained the impression that Lee was impli-
cated, and initiated an investigation to obtain the facts.
The results of the investigation, when they finally arrived, did implicate Lee in wrongdoing. Therefore, in
April 1878, Davidson had Captain Lee brought to trial.
Although acquitted Lee became very vengeful towards
Davidson.[2]

Shortly after he was transferred from Fort Richardson, Captain Baldwin wrote a letter of complaint to the
Commander, Department of Texas, a copy of which is
not available. As a result Davidson received the follow-

---

[2] Davidson ACP file, and Davidson's personal records in the author's file.

ing letter dated February 19, 1878, from the Commander, Department of the Missouri,[3]

Lieut. Col. J. W. Davidson
19th Cavalry, Fort Sill, I.T.
Sir: I am directed by the Department Commander to inform you that the letter of Capt. Theo. A. Baldwin, 10th Cavalry, dated January 10, 1878 and addressed to Asst. Adjt. Genl., Headquarters, Department of Texas, wherein he makes certain allegations against you, and also the charges and specifications preferred against you by the same officer on January 14, 1878, have been received at these Headquarters and that after a careful examination of all the papers he concurs in the opinion of the Acting Judge Advocate of the Department that there is nothing to warrant a trial of the charges preferred, and the allegations made against you, and that they will not be entertained or further action had in them.   E. R. PLATT
Copy to Captain Baldwin   Asst. Adjutant General

One would think that the receipt of such a letter should be enough to put a stop to any further actions of that type. But Baldwin's vengeance remained. Before proceeding it is worthy of note that Baldwin seemed to have trouble with any superior officer of the Tenth Cavalry who demanded adherence to established policies and rules of behavior. That is manifested by a letter written several years earlier, as an endorsement to one of Baldwin's letters of complaint (Baldwin's letters not available). At that time Baldwin was under the command of Major G. W. Schofield, Tenth Cavalry, who was also in temporary command of Fort Sill. The endorsement, dated August 14, 1872, is,[4]

---

[3] Davidson ACP file, and Adjutant General of the Army file of J. W. Davidson court-martial of Oct. 10, 1879.
[4] Copy in the files of the author.

Respectfully forwarded though not considered of sufficient consequence to claim the attention of the Dept. Commander. Captain Baldwin complains of the honor conferred upon him by an increase of his command, which is certainly a novelty. His statement that the enlisted men of his command have been compelled to do *extra* guard and fatigue duty is false, if he means that they have been required to do more than their fair proportion of that duty. Company H, to which he refers as having been at the post 14 days without doing guard duty, did nearly all of the fatigue duty without doing guard duty during that time, and was relieved of guard duty for good reasons. On the 10th instant Capt. Baldwin was relieved from command of E Company as it was found for the interest of the service to make the change owing to the behavior of Capt. Baldwin. This officer is one of three or four of this command whose course, since the change of Post Commanders, has indicated a spirit of petty insubordination. A decided effort will be made at once to prevent further annoyance of this kind.

G. W. SCHOFIELD
Major 10th Cavalry

That letter, incidentally, was written just a few weeks after Grierson moved his headquarters to Fort Gibson, leaving Schofield in command of Fort Sill.

Detachments from Fort Sill were in the field, on patrol, for varying periods of time, and the commanding officer, Colonel Davidson, made a practice of inspecting their encampments from time to time. On one such he felt it appropriate to take the patrol commander to task, which was promptly labeled, by that officer, as harrassment. The following letter [5] of reprimand would not appear to be harassment,

Headquarters, Fort Sill, I.T.

Captain T. A. Baldwin, 10th Cavalry   April 3rd 1878

The Commanding Officer directs me to inform you that on his last visit of inspection to your Camp, that your dress was not that

---

[5] Old Post Records, Fort Sill Museum.

of an officer of the Army. You are directed to wear an Officer's dress in your camp, as well as in the Garrison. Further your attention is especially called to Page 404 Cavalry Tactics, with regard to the saluting of officers, and unless soon complied with by you, the Commanding Officer will drill you, so that you will understand the salute. The habit you have of standing with your hands in your pockets when the Commanding Officer is addressing you, is not the proper attitude, as you must remember in your earlier Soldier days, and will not be tolerated. You will stand at attention when the Commanding Officer has occasion to address you hereafter, and you will regard this letter as an imperative order.   L. WHITALL, Post Adjutant

It was during this same period, in early 1878, that the post was furnished with some comedy relief which occurred while Second Lieutenant Henry O. Flipper, Tenth Cavalry, was officer-of-the-day. Flipper was, incidentally, the first Negro to be graduated from West Point. His first assignment was to the Tenth Cavalry, joining Company A under Captain Nolan, at Fort Concho, Texas. He came under the jurisdiction of Black Jack Davidson when Company A was reassigned to Fort Sill in January of that year. Flipper writes in his memoirs of many interesting and trying experiences while serving with the Tenth. One of these occurred while he was the officer-of-the-day. It seems that the post had an especially nice parade ground, and the commander, Colonel Davidson greatly enjoyed seeing the green grass growing, and insisted upon keeping it in good condition at all times. He had noticed that some worn spots were developing from frequent foot traffic across the parade ground. In an effort to correct the situation the post commander issued an order prohibiting anyone from walking on the grass, but no one paid much attention to it. The commander then posted an order to

the officer-of-the-day to station a sentry at the parade
ground with instructions to arrest any person who
walked on the grass. One morning during Flipper's tour
of duty, just before noon, he received word that the sentry had arrested the post commander's son, and put him
in the guard house. Almost immediately an orderly
arrived and said that the officer-of-the-day was directed
to report to the post commander's quarters.

When Lieutenant Flipper arrived at the commander's
quarters he stepped right into the middle of a family
row. The commander's wife told Flipper to release her
son at once. Davidson countermanded his wife's instructions and said that his son, a lad of about eighteen years
of age, would remain in the guardhouse long enough to
learn a lesson. Mrs. Davidson again demanded that her
husband have her boy released at once. Black Jack replied, "Madam, I'll have you know that I am the commanding officer of this post."

Mrs. Davidson retorted, with considerable heat,
"And I'll have you to understand that I'm your commanding officer."

The spirited exchange continued for some time, with
poor Flipper caught in the middle. A few hours later
the boy was released from the guardhouse, and grew up
to be the father of this biographer.

In July 1878, Captain Baldwin launched a new attack upon his "old enemy," Lieutenant Colonel Davidson. He prepared a list of charges which, for the most
part, accused his commanding officer of harsh treatment, tyrannical character, and demanded a full investigation. These charges included a copy of the letter
of reprimand dated April 3, 1878 (previously quoted),
and were forwarded to the Adjutant General of the

Army, under the following letter, dated July 18, 1878,[6]

> (Through Hdqtrs. Ft. Sill, I.T., and Ajt. Gens., Dept. of Mo.)
> I have the honor herewith to respectfully forward Charges and
> Specifications, preferred against Lieut. Col. J. W. Davidson, 10th
> Cavalry and request that they be tried. Also enclose copy of state-
> ment of Mr. George W. Robson as evidence. [Most likely the
> newspaper editor's statement mentioned earlier]
> T. A. BALDWIN, Capt. 10th Cavalry

The reaction to Baldwin's letter was fast, considering
the channels through which it passed, and the slow
movement of the mails. He received the following reply
from the Headquarters Department of the Missouri,
dated August 12, 1878, through the Commanding Officer Fort Sill,

> Sir: I am directed by the Department Commander to inform
> you that the Charges preferred by you against Lieut. Col. David-
> son have been received, and that it is not considered to be the best
> interests of the Service to bring them to trial, as it is plain they
> have originated from malevolence, rather than from a desire to
> promote the good of the Service. I am also directed by the De-
> partment Commander to call your attention to the impropriety of
> your addressing the letter of transmittal to the Adjutant General
> of the Army. The matter is one with which the Department
> Commander has full power to deal, and these charges will not be
> forwarded. E. R. PLATT, Asst. Adjt. Genl.

As is customary a copy of the foregoing action had
been forwarded to army headquarters in Washington,
for the record. It was reviewed, and the following came
back from the adjutant general of the army, dated
October 12, 1878,

---

[6] In proceedings of Davidson court-martial, Oct. 10, 1879. Copies of this
and the following correspondence form a part of General Davidson's personal
copy of the proceedings.

Commanding General Department of the Missouri
Sir: Referring to your endorsements of Aug. 10, 1878 forwarding appeal of Captain T. A. Baldwin, 10th Cavalry, for redress from certain alleged injuries and injustice done him by his Post Commander, Lieut. Col. J. W. Davidson, 10th Cavalry, whose action has been sustained by you. I have the honor to inform you that the papers have been laid before the General of the Army, and the following is his decision in the case:

"The appeal of Captain T. A. Baldwin is denied. The letter addressed him by order of Lieut. Col. Davidson was mild under the circumstances. Commanding officers of all grades should enforce by orders the discipline of their Command, and Lieut. Col. Davidson was right in calling the attention of Captain Baldwin to an unmilitary dress, and disrespectful manner. The letter of his Adjutant Whitall contains no threat which was not justified by the facts."   E. D. TOWNSEND, Adjutant General

Apparently, some time prior to the receipt of the above letter Captain Baldwin appealed the department commander's decision, for the following letter from the adjutant general of the army, dated October 21, 1878, arrived through channels,

Commanding General Military Division of the Missouri,
Sir: Referring to your endorsement of the 11th instant forwarding Charges and Specifications, 2 sets, preferred by Captain T. A. Baldwin, 10th Cavalry, against Lieut. Col. J. W. Davidson, 10th Cavalry, concurring in the expression of opinion by the Commanding General, Department of the Missouri, that the best interests of the Service do not require that the matter be submitted to a General Court Martial. I have the honor to inform you that the papers have been submitted to the General of the Army, and the following is his decision on the subject:

"This case having been acted on by the Department and Division Commanders infavorably—I deny this appeal from their decision."
          E. D. TOWNSEND, Adjt. Genl. U.S. Army

Copies of all that correspondence were furnished to all interested parties and commands. Evidently advance notification of the contents of the quoted letters from the adjutant general of the army reached Captain Baldwin long before the actual documents arrived at Fort Sill. It was then that Mrs. Baldwin entered the dispute. She wrote a personal letter to the wife of the President of the United States, Rutherford B. Hayes, on October 13, 1878. In it she described Davidson as "nearly always under the influence of alcoholic stimulant." The President forwarded her letter to the Secretary of War on October 28, 1878, with this cryptic note, "I suspect the enclosed requires very little attention. R. B. Hayes"

Under the date of November 13, 1878 the general of the army forwarded that correspondence, through channels, to Captain Baldwin, with the following remarks,

Respectfully referred to Lt. Gen. P. H. Sheridan who will notify Mrs. Baldwin that the meddling with the official action of the Commanding Officer cannot but prejudice the status of her husband. Her acts are his, and he cannot shelter himself behind her petticoats. As the Department Commander has twice decided that the Charges of Captain Baldwin are not worthy of a trial by a General Court Martial and as this discretion is rightly his official prerogative, Capt. Baldwin should be warned to desist and to compel his wife to desist from writing to the wife of the President such a letter as is herein referred to, and that if he subjects the U.S. to the expense of a General Court Martial his own will likely result. W. T. SHERMAN, General

Upon receipt of the foregoing Captain Baldwin originated a reply which stated, among other things,

He holds himself responsible for the statements made by his wife, and is ready to prove their correctness and also the Charges he has made against Lieut. Col. Davidson.

With that parting blast Captain Baldwin seems to have retreated from any further action in this respect.

Since Mrs. Baldwin, in her letter, made the statement that Davidson was nearly always under the influence of liquor, it is, at this juncture, appropriate to back-track a bit, and discuss that particular issue. One should bear in mind that the cavalrymen of the great plains, during the years following the close of the Civil War, were generally classified as, "hard riding, hard fighting and hard drinking" soldiers. While in garrison there probably was a great deal of drinking, since the sutlers' stores dispensed huge quantities of whiskey to both officers and enlisted ranks. However, drunkenness was not widespread. While operating in the field it was customary for those field commanders, of and above the rank of major, to carry a "How Box" in the supply wagon. That was usually the first item unloaded when camp was made each night, and it would be placed in the commander's tent. These How Boxes were beautifully constructed of polished hardwood, about eighteen inches square, and about fifteen inches in depth. Their interiors were partitioned to hold a dozen or more quart bottles of whiskey or whatever hard liquor happened to be available. Upon completion of their evening chores it was the practice of the officers of the detachment to assemble at the commander's tent for a refreshing drink or two.

If one should wonder why such a practice was condoned, just consider what a Captain Bourke, of the Third Cavalry wrote in one of his letters. He said,[7]

To march into battle with banners flying, drums beating and the pulse throbbing with the promptings of honorable ambition and

---

[7] E. L. N. Glass, *History of the Tenth Cavalry.*

enthusiasm, in unison with the roar of artillery, does not call for half the nerve and determination that must be daily exercised to pursue, mile after mile, in such terrible weather, over rugged mountains and through unknown canyons, a foe whose habits of warfare are repugnant to every principle of humanity, and whose presence can be determined solely by the flash of the rifle which lays some poor sentry low, or the whoop and yell which stampeded our stock from the grazing grounds. The life of a soldier, in time of war, has scarcely a compensating feature; but he ordinarily expects palatable food whenever obtainable, and good warm quarters during the winter season. In campaigning against the Indians, if anxious to gain success, he must lay aside every idea of good food and comfortable lodgings, and make up his mind to undergo with cheerfulness privations from which other soldiers would shrink back dismayed. His sole object should be to strike the enemy and to strike hard, and this accomplished should be full compensation for all the privations undergone. With all its advantages this system of Indian warfare is a grand school for the cavalryman of the future, teaching them fortitude, vigilance, self reliance, and dexterity, besides that instruction in handling, marching, feeding, and fighting troops which no school can impart in textbooks.

Is it any wonder that these soldiers welcomed an opportunity to relax over a good stiff drink?

Certainly Davidson was no angel, nor was he a devil. He was as tough as the soldiers he commanded, and was capable of using extremely strong language, when it seemed appropriate. This was well known to all. What was not well known, or was deliberately misunderstood, was the effect of his many bouts with malaria. While in Fort Richardson he had many recurring attacks of the malaria that had plagued him for so long. Subsequent to the retiring board action Davidson resolved to carry on with his duties, regardless of the consequences to him. That may have been unwise since he sometimes endeavored to function while in a feverish condition,

ignoring the surgeon's advice to go to bed. It is certain
that the "Davidson haters" construed those situations as
periods of intoxication. Such a feverish condition often
has an effect similar to intoxication. Then too, such an
interpretation was quite plausible, because Davidson
enjoyed a drink or two as well as any man.

That the year of 1878 was a difficult one for Davidson
is probably very true. The administrative duties of a
command the size of Fort Sill, the maintenance of mul-
tiple patrols in the field at all times, and the harrassment of those trying to bring him to trial, was a heavy
burden indeed. When Captain Baldwin backed out of
the charges and specifications picture, Captain Lee
stepped in. He fired a salvo, apparently through the
post commander. None of that correspondence could
be located, but the following indicates that it was mis-
handled at first, then lost. That stirred up a hornet's
nest, as indicated in the following,

> 3rd endorsement, Fort Leavenworth, October 31, 1878, Re-
> spectfully referred to Comdg. Officer Fort Sill, I.T. for remarks.
> No Charges of which these purport to be copies have been re-
> ceived at these Hd. Qtrs. Attention is invited to the irregularity
> on the part of Captain Lee in forwarding the copies direct.
>   Signed by E. R. Platt, for General Pope

Upon receipt of that latter Colonel Davidson responded, on November 13, 1878, as follows,

> Respectfully returned. The charges which these are a copy were
> handed into my office while I was suffering under a dangerous
> illness, and were held to await my recovery and remarks. My
> public duties just now, owing to preparations of the Indians for
> their hunt, etc., will not admit of my giving all the attention to
> this paper that full and conclusive remarks would require for my
> proper standing in this matter. I forward such few statements as
> I can get right here and earnestly request a Court of Inquiry

upon the subject matter of these charges and that the Court be ordered to express opinions upon the merits of the case and recommend further action if necessary.

Since almost all of the charges leveled against him were based upon drunkenness, Davidson requested the post surgeon to provide him with a statement regarding his several illnesses during the past twelve months. Under the date of November 22, 1878, the surgeon addressed the following to Colonel Davidson,

> In reply to your letter of October 8th 1878, I have the honor to state that from June 16th 1878 to the middle of October you have been the subject of repeated attacks of malarial fever, and that you are now suffering from what are known as the chronic results of that febrile state, namely: derangement of the functions of the liver, spleen and stomach. I believe further that a long residence in this and other malarious districts has rendered your system unduly susceptible to the marsh poison, hence the grave nature of your late attacks, the harassing gastric symptoms attending and the extreme debility following each of these attacks. In regard to the attacks from which you suffered on or about August 2, 1878, I am of the opinion that it was of the nature of a severe but partial heat stroke of the asthenic type, to which you were predisposed by debility resulting from fever, and by the fact that you previously had suffered from sunstroke.
>
> J. W. WILLIAMS, Surgeon U.S.A.
Post Surgeon

On February 1, 1879, Captain Lee resubmitted his charges and specifications against Davidson. Many long months were to elapse before anything further was heard from this action. It was evident that the entire package that Lee had prepared was being given careful scrutiny. Meanwhile the post settled down to the normal routine, which certainly was more than enough to keep the personnel too busy to worry about trivialities.

From Texas to Fort Custer

The shift of the great cattle drives from the Chisholm to the Western trail, that began in late 1877, caused a very crowded condition to exist on the latter trail during most of the summer months. That, quite naturally, threw an extremely heavy burden on the two forts most affected, Griffin and Elliott. The latter named post, situated about twenty-five miles west of the Texas-Oklahoma border, in the Panhandle, bore the brunt of the added patrol load. As a consequence it became necessary to strengthen the garrison by almost doubling its population. Therefore, Black Jack Davidson, and over one-half of the total strength of the Tenth Cavalry, was shifted from Fort Sill to Fort Elliott on January 27, 1879, with Davidson assigned as commanding officer.

Within a short time after he arrived at Fort Elliott, Davidson became involved in a quarrel with the Texas Rangers. The dispute had its inception at Fort Concho in late 1877. According to historical authorities, when Colonel Grierson moved the Tenth Cavalry headquarters to Fort Concho, the status of the Negro troopers in that locality took a sharp nose dive in the eyes of the local community. As one writer expresses it,[1]

> At Fort Concho, under General B. H. Grierson's command, an all time high was reached in the general resentment of Negroes. The Negro troopers were known as "Grierson's Brunettes."

[1] J. Evetts Haley, *Fort Concho and the Texas Frontier*.

Other writers agree on the fact that Grierson was at constant loggerheads with the civil authorities because of his lenient policy regarding soldiers. As a consequence the soldiers from the fort often became embroiled in altercations with the local toughs who frequented the saloons.

In the fall of 1877 Captain John S. Sparks, in command of a company of Texas Rangers, set up camp near Fort Concho. On the night of their arrival several of Sparks' "rough and ready boys" piled into a saloon for drinks, and other diversions. As they danced with the Mexican girls they noticed that Negro soldiers were doing the same. The Rangers didn't like it and proceeded to shoot up the place. The unarmed troopers left, in high dudgeon, and reported the incident to Colonel Grierson. The colonel called upon Captain Sparks for an apology. Sparks resented that, and responded by saying that he and his little company could whip the entire post of Fort Concho. Grierson did not call his bluff. The outraged soldiers, therefore, took matters in their own hands by going back to the saloon, with arms from the fort, expecting that the Rangers might still be there. A gun fight broke out, and caused the death of a bystander. After that Grierson reported the affair to Adjutant General Steele, the head of the Rangers, in Austin, Texas. This resulted in Captain Sparks' dismissal from the Rangers. He was replaced by Captain G. W. Arrington, who was a notorious hothead, with a particular feeling of disdain for the army, and Negro troopers especially.

Early in February 1878, at Fort Concho, a party of cowboys and hunters set upon a Negro sergeant in a saloon, cut the chevrons off his blouse, and ripped the stripes off his pants. After considerable fighting the Negroes were run out of the saloon. They ran to the fort, got their guns and returned to start a fight. One soldier and one civilian were killed. Captain Arrington rounded up his Rangers and marched them to Fort Concho to arrest the sergeant who had allowed the soldiers to have their guns. He marched across the parade ground, whereupon Grierson challenged his right to be there. The Rangers left empty-handed. A short time later, Captain Arrington and his company of Rangers left Fort Concho with orders to establish a station in the general vicinity of Fort Griffin.

Relative quiet prevailed, insofar as the Rangers were concerned, until the winter of 1878-1879. Arrington received a report that the Indians, from their reservations in New Mexico and the Oklahoma Territory, were reported to be in the Texas Panhandle. Captain Arrington led some seventeen Rangers on a scouting mission intended to chase the Indians back to their reservations. They encountered rough going because of the heavy snows, and their tempers began to boil. A small party of Indians was overtaken, and one of them killed. Later on the Rangers came upon a camp of Indians and prepared to attack when a detachment of the Tenth Cavalry, under Captain Nolan, galloped up to protect the Indians. That because it had been the recent practice of the federal government to permit the Indians to hunt in certain parts of Texas, including the Panhandle. Some of the Texans in the region resented that practice, and the Rangers were disposed to kill any Indian they found on Texas soil. Arrington resented what he considered the interference of the Tenth Cavalry from Fort Elliott, and returned to his station with a temper at the boiling point.

A short time later news reached Captain Arrington that the Indians had been depredating in the Panhandle. He, with twenty men, left with forty days' rations and set up camp on Sweetwater Creek a few days later. Shortly after he arrived in the camp, Captain Arrington and his men set out in pursuit of a party of Kiowa Indians, and succeeded in killing one. Almost immediately Captain Nolan with a detachment out of Fort Elliott arrived on the scene. Nolan visited Arrington and told him that the Kiowas were a peaceful hunting party who were operating under his immediate supervision. A bitter argument ensued, with nothing being settled. From that time on many bitter clashes developed between the Rangers and the troopers of the Tenth Cavalry. Finally Black Jack Davidson and Captain Arrington met face to face. At that time Arrington allowed his hot temper, and dislike for the army, to have full control of his many remarks. He stated that he intended to kill every armed Indian that he saw. Davidson bluntly warned him not to do so, and said he would keep his troops in that area to protect peaceful Indians from the unlawful attacks of Rangers and others.

A few days later Arrington wrote the following letter to Davidson, dated June 18, 1879,[2]

Lieut. Col. Davidson, 10th Cavalry
Commanding Post Fort Elliot
Sir: One John Donnelly a clerk in the Post Traders store has said in substance as follows, That you would fire upon me and my men or put us in irons if we should kill or molest any Indians in the Panhandle. This man Donnelly is the one whom you honored as a messenger to me on the day of my arrival here, and for that reason I think his talk should be noticed.

[2] Walter P. Webb, *The Texas Rangers.*

I therefore desire to know whether or not Donnelly expressed your intentions in policy, not that I have any fears of you in the execution of the enterprise, but for the purpose of laying the matter before the Governor and the Legislature of Texas which is now in session.

Black Jack Davidson made no reply to Arrington's letter. He did, however, interrogate Donnelly about his alleged statement to Arrington. Donnelly denied it, and wrote a sworn statement that completely cleared Davidson of any such threats. Davidson, in turn, made a copy of Arrington's letter and, with Donnelly's statement, reported the entire situation to Governor Roberts of Texas. Nothing further came of the incident. Nevertheless, the Rangers stopped harassing the Indians' hunting parties in the Panhandle.

With that problem out of the way Davidson turned his attention to the more important problems connected with patrolling the cattle trails. But that was interrupted when, on June 25, 1879, a communication reached him that he had been promoted to full colonel, to rank from March 20, 1879, and to command the Second Cavalry. He lost no time in accepting that commission by return mail, with the following letter, dated June 25, 1879,

Genl. E. D. Townsend
Adjutant General U.S. Army
General: I have the honor to acknowledge the receipt of my commission of Colonel of the 2nd U.S. Cavalry Regiment, and to accept same.
Herewith please find oath of allegiance to the United States of America.

This was, indeed, great news for all of the Davidsons. First of all, it was a long overdue promotion. It was thirty-four years since he had graduated from the Military Academy at West Point, during which time he had an exemplary record. Since the end of the Civil War he had looked forward to this promotion, feeling all the while that it was just around the corner. Secondly, since the Second Cavalry headquarters was in Fort Custer, Montana, he was now about to move into a climate that should prove beneficial to his health. No record, nor narrative, can possibly give an adequate description of the agonies he had suffered, in recent years, while on duty in Texas and Oklahoma. Ample reason, therefore, for rejoicing in the Davidson household.

One can imagine the multitude of thoughts that raced through the Colonel's mind, when he contemplated a return to the Second Cavalry. It was the regiment to which he had been assigned when promoted to major in 1861. All during the Civil War he was carried on the rolls of the Second as an officer on detached duty. At the expiration of the war he commanded the regiment for about eighteen months, until appointed a lieutenant colonel in the Tenth Cavalry. Naturally he was fond of that regiment because so many happy experiences were associated with it. Then too, it would be a decided change from the exceptionally rigorous duties of the last ten years, and probably would be more pleasant. He also looked forward to the opportunity, thus afforded, to see old friends, many of whom he had not seen in a great many years. The current commander of the Second Cavalry, Colonel Innis N. Palmer, who was retiring because of age, was an old and trusted friend.

That the Davidsons were eager to leave Fort Elliott is an understatement. They proceeded to set records for packing out of a post of duty. Since his orders contained all the necessary authorizations, there was no reason for delay. Davidson turned the command of the post over to the next senior officer of the fort on June 26, 1879, and the Davidsons set out on their long journey. The orders allowed a short stop en route to the new post, at a place of their choosing, which was Manhattan, Kansas, where the family home was located. However, that stop would be controlled by the length of time needed to reach there from Fort Elliott. That stage of the journey was slow, since there were no railroads available, and they had to travel by means of an army wagon train until a rail terminal was reached. As it turned out, they could afford about one week in Manhattan, which was utilized in seeing old friends and viewing the changes in the city that had occurred during their long absence.

In mid-July Colonel Davidson and family started out on the long trip to Fort Custer. The actual number of miles to be covered on that journey is not known, but fairly close estimates put it near eighteen hundred. From Manhattan they took the train to Kansas City, Missouri, where a steamer was boarded for the long ride up the Missouri River to Bismarck, North Dakota. At that point they changed to another steamer, the Rose Bud, for the last leg of their river traveling. This steamer took them further up the Missouri, to the confluence of the Yellowstone and Missouri rivers, thence on the Yellowstone to Miles City, Montana. At each terminal point it was necessary to lay over for a few days waiting for a sailing. From Miles City the trip to Fort Custer was by stagecoach. Relative to their arrival in Miles City, the following news item from the August 7, 1879, edition of the *Yellowstone Journal* is of interest,

QUICKEST TRIP ON RECORD

The steamer Rose Bud arrived from Fort Keogh on Monday, having made the round trip from Bismarck to Fort Keogh and return in seven days and twelve hours. This is by far the fastest time ever made by any steamer, and Capt. Joe Todd and the Rose Bud are entitled to the champion flag. The Rose Bud departed for Terry's landing with a full load of freight. Thirty six horses, two cows, two coops of carrier pigeons and a full list of passengers, together with a large party of United States engineers who go to Buffalo Rapids to clean out the obstructions in the River. Among the Rose Bud's passengers were Col. Davidson and family, consisting of wife, two daughters, and a son.

Since the steamers had to go against the current, traveling upriver, their movement must have been quite slow, regardless of the speed run reported in the foregoing article. Therefore, it is estimated that the entire trip from Manhattan to Fort Custer must have taken at least four weeks.

On August 11, 1879, Colonel Davidson arrived at Fort Custer, and without delay assumed command of the Second Cavalry and the fort.[3] He found everything to be in the first class condition that he had anticipated, because his predecessor, Colonel Palmer,[4] was an old-line cavalry officer whose policies coincided with those of Colonel Davidson. The next few weeks were fully occupied with familiarizing himself with the activities of the post, and making official calls upon the senior commanders at other, not-too-far-distant forts. Then too, he made inspection trips to outlying posts that were manned by Second Cavalry troops, and for the purpose of becoming familiar with the surrounding countryside.

Meanwhile the slow-moving wheels of army proc-

---

[3] Regimental Returns, Second Cavalry. National Archives.

[4] Joseph I. Lambert, *One Hundred Years with the Second Cavalry.*

essing finally brought to a head the long-standing dispute between Davidson and the three officers of his former command, Captains Baldwin, Lee and Nolan. He received orders to proceed to Fort Riley, Kansas, to appear before a general court-martial that had been designated to try the case. Although somewhat concerned about the outcome, he did firmly believe he would be cleared of all charges. Certainly, he welcomed the opportunity to thrash out the entire situation in the impartial atmosphere of a court-martial. Until that occurred there would be some sort of stain on his otherwise clear and illustrious record. His mode of traveling back to Kansas was somewhat faster than the one just completed, since he was alone, and the downstream current moved steamers ahead at a greater rate of speed.

The court convened at Fort Riley on October 10, 1879, and after a trial lasting several days, published their findings. They are listed, in a very abbreviated form, as follows:

General Court Martial Orders, No. 72
    Colonel John W. Davidson, 2nd Cavalry
Headquarters Department of the Missouri
    Assistant Adjutant General's Office
             Fort Leavenworth, Kansas, October 20, 1879
Before a General Court Martial which convened at Fort Riley, Kansas, October 10, 1879, pursuant to paragraph 1, Special Orders No. 183, current series, from these Headquarters, and of which Colonel Israel Vodges, 1st Artillery, is President, was arraigned and tried: Colonel John W. Davidson, 2nd Cavalry.

CHARGE 1ST – Drunkenness on duty in violation of the 38th Article of War.
    Specification 1st (briefed).[5] Drunk on duty in command of Fort Richardson, Texas, on August 22, 1877.

---

[5] The term "briefed" as used here and below, refers to briefing of specifications by the author.

Specification 2nd (briefed). Drunk on duty in command of
Fort Richardson, Texas, on January 11, 1878.

CHARGE 2ND – Conduct to the prejudice of good order and military discipline.

Specification (briefed). Rendered himself sick and unfit for
duty by the intemperate use of drugs and stimulants, from
October 10 to October 30, 1878.

CHARGE 3RD – Conduct unbecoming an officer and a gentleman.

Specification 1st (briefed). On August 22, 1877, at Fort Richardson was drunk and needed the assistance of a Lieutenant
Jouett to reach his quarters. Later at Fort Sill, on December
8, 1878, stated that he would take action against Lieutenant
Jouett for talking about the incident.

Specification 2nd (briefed). Almost a duplicate of the first
specification.

Specification 3rd (briefed). Similar to the above except that he
requested Lieutenant Jouett to suppress his knowledge of the
affair on December 9, 1878.

Specication 4th (briefed). Made a false statement about the
charges and specifications in his possession, and tried to with-
hold them from the adjutant general, about November 13,
1878.

Specification 5th (briefed). On October 10, 1878, received a
copy of the charges and failed to enter them in the post
records.

Specification 6th (briefed). Had employed a Sergeant Gibson
to spy on the officers of the command, then denied it before
a court-martial of Captain P. L. Lee, 10th Cavalry, on
November 18, 1878.

Specification 7th (briefed). Stated before the officers that he
would not permit Sergeant Gibson to act as a detective to
obtain evidence against Captain Lee, on May 5, 1878.

Specification 8th (briefed). Sent Sergeant Gibson to Fort Griffin, Texas, to obtain evidence against Captain Lee, on May
5, 1878.

Specification 9th (briefed). Confined a civilian, Joseph Wright,
in the guardhouse to oppress him, on August 13, 1878.

Specification 10th (briefed). Issued an order for detached

service of a private to take a wagon to Caddo, Indian Territory, to transport the private property of an officer, under
the guise of official business, on November 12, 1878.

The charges and specifications tried by the court were
developed from the ones that had been submitted by
Captain Lee. The trial lasted for seven days during
which time there were twelve witnesses for the prosecution and none for the defense. Of the witnesses for the
prosecution, eight were army officers including Captains Baldwin and Lee, two were civilians, and two
army doctors including the post surgeon at Fort Sill.
In general the testimony of six of the eight army officers
was favorable to Davidson, as was that of the civilians
and doctors. Captain Baldwin's testimony for the prosecution was very weak to begin with, and broke down
under cross-examination. Captain Lee did his best to
present a strong case against Davidson, but under cross-
examination it was clearly demonstrated that he was
acting from animus. It was also brought out that most
of the charges and specifications, as originally submitted
by him, were based upon hearsay. The two army doctors testified as to Davidson's serious illness at some of
the times when he was accused of drunkenness.

It is evident that both Colonel Davidson and his
counsel recognized the utter weakness of the prosecution's case. Therefore, the counsel for the defense, Captain William V. Richards, made this closing statement,

Gentlemen of the Court. The accused, by the advice of his
Counsel, having full confidence in the justice of his cause, and
believing that he has not been injured by the testimony of the
prosecution in any manner, submits his case upon the showing of
the prosecution and asks from you an honorable acquittal.

The court threw out the first specification of the first

charge. On the remaining charges and specifications they found the defendant "Not Guilty," and acquitted him. The convening authority reviewed the entire proceedings, and endorsed them with the following remarks, under date of October 20, 1879,

> The proceedings, findings and acquittal in the case of Colonel John W. Davidson, 2nd Cavalry, are approved, except the action of the Court in throwing out, of its motion, the 1st Specification of 1st Charge, which is disapproved.

By its action the court-martial board served to erase all possible stain from Colonel Davidson's record which is, of course, extremely important to a military officer. Any uneasiness he may have had about the case, during the preceding year or so, was completely dissipated, and he could now feel comfortable. He personally thanked each member of the court, including the judge advocate, for their proper and impartial conduct of the trial. No time was lost in starting the return trip to Fort Custer, where he arrived on December 3, 1879. The Christmas celebration in the Davidson household that year must have been especially joyous.

The writer of this biography has, in his files, an exact copy of the entire proceedings and findings. Although the charges and specifications were well written, it is not surprising that they could not withstand an attack by the counsel for the defense. Captain Nolan, incidentally, did not testify at the trial. It is not known whether Captain Lee was reprimanded for bringing the case to trial, since his motivations seemed to be more malicious than otherwise, but it appears that he should have.

In commenting further upon that trial, and the motivations of those few who were "out for Davidson's scalp," it is conceivable that they sought to enhance their own positions in the process. During those exceedingly difficult years, of this nation's history, the officers of the army spent long, hard years on the frontier under constantly dangerous conditions. All the while they would hope and pray for promotions or assignments to more desirable localities. Since the total strength of the army, for more than twenty years, never exceeded twenty-five thousand, promotions were exceedingly slow. In fact there are a few cases where officers remained in the rank of lieutenant for as much as fifteen years. It was only natural, therefore, that almost every officer was sensitive to the assignments of his fellows, for fear that favoritism would give them an unfair advantage. And that often happened, causing jealousies to be widespread. Under those circumstances the junior officers often became intensely loyal to, and curried favor with, those senior officers who might help to further their careers. That situation prevailed when Davidson took command of the Tenth Cavalry, and became closely associated with those officers who had "hitched their stars" to the benevolence of Colonel Grierson. Undoubtedly they viewed Davidson as a threat to their future well-being. Conceivably Captains Baldwin and Lee may have been so motivated and, therefore, endeavored to have Davidson removed through the actions of a court-martial.

Fort Custer was a comparatively new post, having been built in 1877 on the Big Horn River, at the mouth of the Little Big Horn. At the same time Fort Keogh was established on the Yellowstone River, at the mouth of the Tongue. They were ordered into being because, following the disastrous defeat of Custer, the Indian depredations in the area had increased at an alarming rate. During these years, in addition to some infantry, both of these posts were manned, chiefly, by the Second Cavalry, which had been relocated from its long-time base in the Department of the Platte. Companies C, D, K, and M, with the headquarters band and staff were stationed at Fort Custer, and Companies A, B, E, and I located at Fort Keogh. The primary responsibility of the Second Cavalry was to police the entire area. They watched the countryside for the possible return from Canada of Sitting Bull and, at the same time, drove renegades back to their reservations. Colonel Davidson's command, in addition to the cavalry regiment, included the District of the Yellowstone and Fort Custer. It was a large scale responsibility, since it involved thousands of square miles of territory, including Yellowstone National Park.

In the summer of 1879, just before the arrival of Davidson, Colonel Nelson A. Miles was directed by General Terry, the departmental commander, to assemble a force strong enough to drive a large band, consisting of some two thousand warriors belonging to Sitting Bull, back to their home bases in Canada. These warriors had been marauding as far south as the Missouri River. Miles set out with seven companies of the Second Cavalry, plus several companies of infantry, and succeeded in chasing the hostiles back across the border. It was hoped by General Terry that the action would cause Sitting Bull to remain in Canada, but not so. Sitting Bull's warriors felt it necessary to follow the buffalo when they moved south, and soon, again, crossed the border and made numerous raids upon small settlements. Sergeant Glover, Second Cavalry, was sent out to pursue a small party of marauding Indians, on February 3, 1880. He had charge of a detachment of fifteen men, who slogged their way through heavily falling snow and temperatures of fifty degrees below zero. They found the hostiles' camp on February 7th and immediately attacked. The sergeant sent one man back for reinforcements, while he laid siege on the camp. Later, when Captain Snyder with Company F, 11th Infantry, arrived, he found Sergeant Glover barely holding on against a very large number of Indians. One wonders how these men could even survive in that weather, and attack a group of hostiles much larger than themselves.

In March 1880, Lieutenant J. H. Coale, in command of Company C, and Captain Eli Huggins, in command of Company E, both 2nd Cavalry, set out, separately, in pursuit of numerous hostiles. The Indians led them through the Bad Lands, across the Rosebud and Tongue rivers toward the Powder River. They were forced to march as much as fifty miles a day, and their forage consisted of nothing but grass. Because of this poor forage several of the horses reached the limit of their endurance, and had to be abandoned. The last thirty-six hours of the pursuit found both detachments with nothing to eat but coffee, hard bread, and a small amount of meat from buffalo that had been killed by the Indians. The two companies had set out separately, but joined for an attack upon the Indians near the Powder River on April 1, 1880. They caught up with the hostiles at about two thirty p.m., and charged headlong into their midst separating the Indians from their mounts. As a result they captured forty-six ponies and five Indians.

The remaining Indians managed to escape during darkness. Both Captain Huggins and 2nd Lieutenant Lloyd M. Brett were awarded Congressional Medals of Honor for their bravery during the fracas.

Those two incidents are characteristic of the activities of the Second Cavalry during Colonel Davidson's command of the regiment. The troops of the Second were constantly chasing marauding Indians and engaging in similar skirmishes, until Sitting Bull finally surrendered on July 19, 1881. One historical writer describes those activities in the following terms,[6]

> Great credit must be given to the troops of the Second Cavalry for their fortitude against Sitting Bull during the winter (1880-1881). Much of the time during their movements the thermometer registered from 20 to 50 degrees below zero. They endured every hardship cheerfully and prepared with vigor to meet the hostile Indians.

Although constant attention had to be paid to the hit-and-run tactics of the hostile Indians, the attacks always occurred far enough from Fort Custer that its occupants were not endangered. Consequently, the life at the post was peaceful and pleasant. Parties, picnics and excursions were frequent, thus providing an enjoyable social life for the residents. It was at one of those affairs that a dashing young lieutenant, Curtis B. Hoppin, 2nd Cavalry, became acquainted with the colonel's oldest daughter, Elizabeth. He forthwith launched a whirlwind campaign to win her hand in marriage. That he was successful can be attested to by the gala wedding that was held on the post in the early spring of 1880. Lieutenant Hoppin was serving as the regimental quartermaster at the time.

---

[6] Joseph I. Lambert, *One Hundred Years with the Second Cavalry*.

A post the size of Fort Custer necessarily employed a number of civilians, and the largest group at that post was the freight section. Since the railroads had not penetrated that far in the northwest, all of the freight for Custer was transported by river steamer and wagon train. Steamers unloaded their cargo at the nearest river port where it was picked up and moved to the fort by wagon train. That being a very busy activity there were always openings for young and vigorous men. The Colonel, therefore, had the post quartermaster, who had responsibility for the freight activity, make job offers to his two sons who were living in Kansas. They both accepted, and the older one started as a teamster while the younger one started as a packer. Their names were William and George respectively. In a short while George, the father of this writer, was promoted to freight agent. Perhaps some would look upon this employment situation as a form of nepotism, because the colonel had influence over the post quartermaster. On the other hand, both William and George were grown men who, according to the post records, performed their jobs satisfactorily. Who is to judge?

Another occurrence, of great interest to this writer, was when the officers of the regiment prepared a petition to have George Davidson, then twenty-two years of age, appointed second lieutenant in the Second Cavalry. Every officer in the regiment signed that document, and forwarded it through official channels to army headquarters in Washington.[7] This was not unusual since it was the practice at that time for the army to appoint a few second lieutenants from civil life each

[7] Davidson ACP file.

year, in addition to the graduates from West Point. As post commander, Colonel Davidson was required to place his endorsement on the petition, and forward it to the next higher authority. Of course his endorsement was favorable. As any proud father would, Davidson then sat down and wrote this personal letter to the adjutant-general of the army, under the date of July 5, 1880,

> My Dear General Drum: By this time you will have received a petition from the officers of the 2nd Cavalry to have my son, Geo. K. Davidson, appointed in the Army from civil life, and assigned to this Regiment. This is the spontaneous act of my comrades – I ask you who knew me in California to place this matter before the General of the Army in as favorable light as you can consistently do, and ask his interest in the matter. My father was a Captain of the 3rd Artillery, and I believe the General served with him in Florida.

The colonel's eagerness to have his son appointed is easily understood when it is realized that it always had been family tradition for a son of each generation to become an officer in the army, but neither of the two had gone to West Point. Many favorable endorsements accompanied the original petition, and several personal letters of recommendation were sent to Washington by prominent individuals. As was customary at the time, the petition moved slowly through channels, and arrived at headquarters on December 22, 1880, and was filed with this notation,

> This letter is placed on file for use when 2nd Lieutenants are to be appointed, which will not be until May of 1881.[8]

That filing was customary, since appointments from civil life were never made until it was known how many

----
[8] *Ibid.*

A Vacation Group at Yellowstone Park, 1880
Standing: John W. Davidson and Lieutenant Curtis B. Hoppin
Seated: Eddie Davidson, Letta Davidson, Mrs. Davidson, and the
recently married Mrs. Hoppin, formerly Elizabeth Davidson

would graduate from West Point each year. Under the circumstances, however, it is probable that George Davidson would have been appointed, had it not been for a fatal accident which occurred a few months later.

In the late spring of 1880 Colonel Davidson, at the head of a large detachment from his regiment, made a tour of inspection through many areas of the territory for which he was responsible. The purpose was two-fold: to familiarize himself with the general layout of the country, and to inspect the several military outposts which were manned by troops of the Second Cavalry. In the process he thoroughly explored Yellowstone Park, to see if any damage had been done by hostile Indians. This tour through the Park established a first. Colonel Davidson was the first Army commander to lead his troops through that park. He liked what he saw so well that he brought his family, and a few close friends, to the park during the summer of 1880, for a vacation.

When the new year of 1881 dawned, Colonel Davidson received a directive from General Terry, the departmental commander, to establish a memorial that would commemorate Custer's last stand. He assigned a work detail from Troop C, Second Cavalry, with Lieutenant Charles F. Roe in command, and the freight agent, George Davidson, as superintendent of the over-all operation. Work was begun just as soon as possible. Since the site had been selected, in the Little Big Horn battlefield, on a hill just six feet from where the remains of Custer had been found, no time was lost in proceeding. However, it developed into a large scale undertaking after the decision was made to collect the remains of all the officers and men, for interment at the base of the monument. The task was completed and the monument dedicated in July 1881. However, most of the work was completed under the supervision of Lieutenant Roe, because George Davidson was forced to withdraw from the project, for reasons that will be explained in the following paragraphs.

On February 8, 1881, Colonel Davidson, accompanied by the post quartermaster, Lieutenant Hoppin, set out on a routine tour of inspection of the immediate countryside. It was an extremely cold day, with the ground frozen and iced over in many spots. While riding along the edge of a steep-sided ravine Davidson's horse slipped and tumbled down the ravine, landing on top of the colonel. Two of Davidson's ribs were broken, and his body badly bruised. He was carried back to the fort and the post surgeon set the ribs and administered treatment for the bruises and lacerations on his body. Within a few days Davidson got out of bed and attempted to carry on with his duties as post commander. Although in considerable pain he carried on for the next few months, with his strength and general health slowly worsening. By the first week in May he felt himself to be unfit to continue as regimental commander, and applied for an extended leave of absence. The surgeon's report, dated May 9, 1881, read as follows,

> Colonel J. W. Davidson, of the 2nd Regiment of Cavalry, having applied for a Certificate on which to ground an application for a leave of absence, I do hereby certify that I have carefully examined this officer and find that he is suffering from frequent and severe attacks of *sub-acute gastritis;* and also from *general nervous debility,* the result of his horse having fallen upon him on the 8th of February, 1881, and that in consequence thereof, he is in

my opinion unfit for duty. I further declare my belief that he will not be able to resume his duties in a less period than *one year;* and also that a change of climate is necessary to prevent permanent disability.   JAMES C. MERRILL
Capt. & Asst. Surgeon USA

On May 21, 1881, Colonel Davidson, his wife and two of his sons, Edward and George, started out from Fort Custer to go to the family home in Manhattan, Kansas. As usual the journey was long and tiresome. They were able to travel a short distance by rail, but most was by steamer on the Yellowstone, Missouri and Mississippi rivers. They arrived in St. Paul, Minnesota, on June 21, 1881. Since Davidson was completely tired out from the rigors of the trip, the family checked into the Merchants Hotel to let the colonel rest up for the remainder of the trip home. It was fortunate, indeed, that George Davidson had resigned from his position as freight agent at Fort Custer, in order to accompany his father and mother. Edward was a mere lad in his early teens, and ill-equipped to care for the multitude of details that were necessary for the well-being of his father. Immediately upon arrival in St. Paul, George located the best doctor in the city to minister to the medical needs of the colonel. Unfortunately, however, the trip from Fort Custer had been so completely exhausting that Colonel Davidson was unable to regain any of the strength that was lost prior to his departure from the fort. At five a.m. on June 26, 1881, Colonel John W. Davidson breathed his last. His son, who had been so attentive to his father's comfort, was at his bedside all during the final hours. The colonel was conscious most of the time, and seemed to know that he was nearing the end. He devoted as much time as his strength would allow to giving George instructions on what should be done after his death. Since the colonel had drawn no will, these pertained to the disposition of property, burial instructions, etc. One of the several items covered was this,

> George, I want my saber, the presentation one, to remain in the possession of the Davidson family, passing from the oldest son to his oldest son. With that understanding, I want it to be loaned to the Smithsonian Institution, for display.

As of the date of this writing that saber is proudly displayed in the Smithsonian Institution, in Washington, D.C.

The St. Paul *Pioneer Press,* issue of June 27, 1881, had a news item which announced the death of Colonel Davidson and gave an outline of his career. The final paragraph of that item reads as follows,

> The deceased was much beloved, and though a strict disciplinarian – Black Jack, the men used to call him, was so just withal and so thoroughly the soldier gentleman that none were found who did not do him honor, and few but loved him as a friend.

Upon receipt of the sad news General Terry ordered a guard of honor to be sent from Fort Snelling, to escort the remains to St. Louis, Missouri, for burial. The city of St. Louis, which knew Davidson well, went all-out to do him honor in the burial ceremonies. The newspaper coverage was elaborate and praiseworthy. The funeral procession, with several troops of cavalry in full-dress uniforms, was several blocks long. Colonel Davidson's body was laid to rest in the Bellefontaine Cemetery, in St. Louis, on June 29, 1881. It was moved to the Arlington National Cemetery, in Arlington, Virginia, on February 28, 1911. Thus, Colonel John W. Davidson, United States Army, finally returned to the Virginia soil which gave him birth.

Many articles were published in tribute to Colonel Davidson, but the best probably is this one, taken from the Fort Custer announcement of his death, Orders No. 26, dated June 30, 1881,

He gave his life to the service of his country, and was distinguished for his devotion to duty, and the profession of his choice.

He was always a courteous kindly gentleman, and will long be remembered for his many excellent qualities. The badge of mourning will be worn by all officers of the Regiment, for 30 days.

Epilogue

General John W. Davidson was born into a military family and his entire early life was one that would fit him to be a soldier in the service of the United States. Probably that was the goal of most young lads of the time, when this country was forging its destiny through the force of arms. With such a beginning, plus the training of the Military Academy at West Point, he developed a fierce loyalty to his flag. That was amply demonstrated when he defied family traditions, at the outbreak of the Civil War, and remained with the Union Army.

He was a soldier who believed in force, the kind of force that stands for moral restraint, respect for laws, enforcement of discipline, and everything that makes a man into an effective soldier. He could neither understand nor stand "boot licking," "mollycoddling" or "pussy-footing," since they were morally wrong, and made cowards out of otherwise good soldiers.

While Davidson was strict and exacting, and, as is natural to all men in responsible positions, sometimes irritable, he was never tyrannical or unjust. He was ruled by a sense of firmness and justice, which are the attributes of a good military leader. He demanded results, and in his intensity of purpose he could not tolerate subordinate officers who did not measure up to the high performance standards that he himself always endeavored to meet. In naval parlance, General Davidson always "ran a taut ship." And, in the navy the taut ship was always the happiest and most efficient. Withal, he was considerate of the soldiers' welfare, and never exposed them to dangers that he, himself, would endeavor to avoid. As a cavalry leader he lived up to the traditions of cavalrymen, in that he always *led* his troops into battle, he avoided *sending* them whenever possible. That is the opposite of infantry leaders, in that they usually *sent* their troops into battle.

Most of Davidson's officers regarded him highly, while some did resent what they labeled his unreasonable demands. Nevertheless, the esprit-de-corps, effectiveness, and record of accomplishment of the Tenth Cavalry was never higher than when it was under his command, nor were the number of courts-martial and desertions lower. Many tributes were paid to him, on various occasions, by the enlisted men under his command. What more fitting tribute than the one by his Civil War orderly, Police Officer William Sharpenburg, of the St. Louis police force, at the time of the general's death. In an article of June 29, 1881, in the *St. Louis Republican,* he said, "Davidson was a gallant Commander." By all standards of measurement, General Davidson was a good soldier, loyal to his country, and a gentleman.

Maps of Western Activities of General John W. Davidson

1846–1874

Twentieth century communities are included for reference and are shown in brackets ( ).

←----→ Routes

Map drawn by Clifford Donahue

Copyright, 1974 The Arthur H. Clark Company

Expedition From Fort Sonoma To Clear Lake, May 1850

Ukiah

Clear Lake

Skirmish May 17

Action May 15

Marysville

Yuba R.

Sacramento R.

Bear R.

Cache Cr.

Battle May 20

American R.

Russian R.

Ft. Ross

Santa Rosa

Putah Cr.

Napa R.

Sacramento

Napa

Ft. Sonoma

San Francisco

0 10 20 miles 40

The Red River War Sept.– Nov. 1874

Colo.

Cimarron R.

Kansas

New Mexico

North Canadian R.

Ft. Supply

Mustard Cr.

Canadian R.

Ft. Elliott

Washita R.

Elk Cr.

(Amarillo)

North Fork

Wichita Agency (Anadarko)

Llano Estacado Or Staked Plains

Salt Fork

Prairie Dog Fork

Wichita Mts.

Ft. Sill

Lawton

Texas

Red R.

(Wichita Falls)

0 10 20 30 40 50 miles 100

(Main map)

Davidson's new route to Salt Lake

Owens Lake

Nevada

Utah

Colorado

Fishers Peak

Raton Pass

Death Valley

Cantonment Burgwin

Taos

Action of Cieneguilla, 1854

Okla.

Expedition to explore Owens Lake, 1859

Kern R.

So. Fork

Grand Canyon of Colorado R.

(Bakersfield)

Santa Fe

(Mojave)

Llano Estacado

(Barstow)

(Needles)

Colorado R.

Arizona

New Mexico

Albuquerque

Anton Chico

Ft. Tejon

(Tejon Pass)

Route of Kearny's expedition to California, 1846

Santa Barbara

California

Ft. Sumner

Pecos R.

Los Angeles

(Indio)

(Blythe)

Salton Sea

Socorro

R. Ruidoso

San Juan Capistrano

Ft. Craig

Ft. Stanton

R. Hondo

Warner Ranch

(Phoenix)

Salt R.

Black R.

San Francisco R.

Camp Ojo Caliente

R. Felix

(Escondido)

San Felipe Cr.

Carizo Cr.

Nov. 24

(El Centro)

Gila R.

Camp San Carlos

Blue R.

Gila R.

Oct. 20

R. Penasco

San Pasqual

San Diego

Yuma

Copper Mines

7 Rivers

Expedition to Delaware Cr., 1855

Pacific Ocean

Baja California

Gila R.

Santa Cruz R.

San Pedro R.

San Simon R.

(Silver City)

Ft. Thorn

Pope's Wells

Tucson

(Lordsburg)

Las Cruces

R. Azul

Sonora

Calabasas Ranch Camp

Camp San Simon

Ft. Fillmore

Delaware Cr.

Texas

Nogales

Ft. Buchanan

Camp Moore

Ft. Bliss

El Paso

Camp Santa Cruz

Chihuahua

miles

0 50 100 200

Career Chronology
Bibliography and Index

Chronology of the Career of
Major General John W. Davidson

A brief outline from information furnished by the Adjutant General's office, United States Army.

1825, August 14 – born in Fairfax County, Virginia.

1841, July 1 – appointed Cadet, U.S. Military Academy, West Point, New York.

1845, July 1 – graduated; appointed Brevet Second Lieutenant, First U.S. Dragoons.

1845-1846 – on frontier duty at Fort Leavenworth, Kansas.

1846 – at Fort Crawford, Wisconsin.

1846, April 21 – commissioned Second Lieutenant, First Dragoons.

1846-1848 – War with Mexico: with the Army of the West. Engagements in California: Dec. 6, 1846, Battle of San Pasqual; Jan. 8, 1847, Passage of the San Gabriel River; Jan. 9, 1847, Battle of the Plains of the Mesa.

1848, January 8 – commissioned First Lieutenant, First Dragoons.

1848-1849 – on frontier duty, Los Angeles, California.

1849-1850 – at Sonoma, California; engaged in action at Clear Lake, May 15, 1850; at Russian River and at Sacramento River.

1850 (late) – on recruiting service.

1850, December 1 – to Quartermaster, First Dragoons.

1851, January 4 – to Adjutant, First Dragoons.

1851, to September 30 – in garrison at Jefferson Barracks, Missouri; and frontier duty at Fort Leavenworth, Kansas.

1851 (late)-1853 – at Fort Snelling, Minnesota.

1853-1854 – at Cantonment Burgwin, New Mexico; commanded the Action of Cieneguilla against Jicarilla Apache Indians, Mar. 30, 1854; at Rayado, Santa Fe, and Fort Thorn, New Mexico.

1855, January 20 – commissioned Captain, First Dragoons.

1855-1856 – at Fort Fillmore and Fort Stanton, New Mexico. Commanded the expedition to open the route from Fort Stanton to the Pecos River at the Texas border.

1857 – at Fort Buchanan, New Mexico.

1857-1858 – on scouting expeditions in New Mexico.

1858-1859 – on march to Fort Tejon, California.

1859 – commanded expedition to explore Owens Lake and River.

1859-1860 – at Fort Tejon, California.

1860-1861 – conducted recruits to California; then at Fort Tejon.

1861, November 14 – commissioned Major, Second Cavalry.

1861 November to 1862 March – engaged in defenses of Washington, D.C.

1862, February 3 – Brevet Brigadier General, U.S. Volunteers.

1862 March-July – with Army of the Potomac in the Virginia Peninsular Campaign. Apr. 5, Action of Lees Mills; May 24, Action of Mechanicsville; June 27, Battle of Gaines Mill; June 28, Action of Goldings Farm; June 29, Battle of Savage Station; June 30, Battle of Glendale.

1862 August to November 13 – command of St. Louis District of Missouri.

1863, to February 23 – command of Army of Southeast Missouri; destined to move against Little Rock.

1863, to June 6 – command of St. Louis District of Missouri, and directing movements of troops of the District at Pilot Knob, Fredericktown, and Cape Girardeau; and pursuit of the enemy during Marmaduke's raid into Missouri.

1863, to September 10 – command of Cavalry Division in movement upon Little Rock, Arkansas; Aug. 29, action of Brownsville; Aug. 27, assault on and capture of Bayou Meto; Aug. 29, Action of Ashley's Mills; Sept. 10, Action of Little Rock.

1864, to June – Chief of Cavalry, Military Division of West Mississippi, and West Division Cavalry Bureau.

1864, to November 24 – in command of Cavalry expedition from Baton Rouge to Pascagoula.

1865, to January 3 – Chief of Cavalry, Military Division of West Mississippi.

1865, March 13 – Brevet Major General, U.S. Volunteers and U.S. Army.

1865, to July 17 – command of District of Natchez, Mississippi.

1866, to January 17 – command of Southern District of Mississippi.

1866, to June 1 – command of Second Cavalry, Fort Riley, Kansas.

1866, to September 2 – on tour of Inspection in the Department of Missouri.

1866, to November 1 – in command of Second Cavalry, Fort Riley, Kansas.

1866, December 1 – commissioned Lieutenant Colonel, Tenth U.S. Cavalry.

1867, to December 28 – Acting Inspector General, Department of the Missouri.

1868, to June – on leave of absence.

1868 June to 1871, January 1 – Professor of Military Science and Tactics at the State Agricultural College, Manhattan, Kansas.

1871 to 1873, February 10 – in command of Camp Supply, Indian Territory.

1873 to 1875, March 27 – in command of Tenth Cavalry and of Fort Sill, Indian Territory; led an expedition in the field from Sept. 10 to Oct. 19, 1874.

1875, to August 5 – in command of Fort Griffin, Texas.

1876, to December 6 – on leave of absence.

1876, December 20 to 1878, January 19 – in command of Fort Richardson, Texas, and of the District of Upper Brazos.

1879, to January 27 – in command of Fort Sill, Indian Territory.

1879, March 20 – commissioned Colonel, Second Cavalry.

1879, to June 26 – in command of Fort Elliott, Texas.

1879, June 26 – departure for Fort Custer, Montana.

1879 October-November – before Court-Martial and on Court-Martial duty.

1881, to May 21 – in command of Second Cavalry, District of the Yellowstone, and of Fort Custer, Montana.

1881, to June 26 – on sick leave.

1881, June 26 – died at the age of 58.

Bibliography

OFFICIAL ARMY AND GOVERNMENT RECORDS

National Archives: Appointment, Commission and Personal File, J. W. Davidson.

National Archives: War Department Records, Adjutant General's Office, Group 94: Reports from the Department of New Mexico, 1854-1858.

National Archives: Post Returns of: Camp Supply, Okla., 1870-1880; Fort Buchanan, Ariz., 1856-1862; Fort Gibson, Okla., 1870-1880; Fort Fillmore, New Mex., 1851-1862; Fort Richardson, Tex., 1870-1880; Fort Sill, Okla., 1870-1880; Fort Custer, Mont., 1879-1881.

National Archives: Regimental Returns of: First Dragoons, 1851-1859; Second Cavalry, 1870-1890; Tenth Cavalry, 1867-1880.

Secretary of War, Annual Report, 1857, pp. 212-216: an article on Popes Wells.

United States, 49th Congress, 1st session, Senate Report 1306 (June 10, 1886); and House Report 2943 (June 22, 1886).

Fort Sill, Oklahoma: Fort Sill Museum, Old Post Records.

NEWSPAPERS AND PERIODICALS

Arkansas, Little Rock: Arkansas Gazette, 1964-1965.

California: Los Angeles Star, 1858-1860.

Illinois: Chicago Times, 1863.

Minnesota, St. Paul: Pioneer Press, 1881.

Missouri, St. Louis: Missouri Democrat, 1863-1864.

———: St. Louis Union, 1863-1864.

Montana, Miles City: Yellowstone Journal, August 7, 1879.

New York City: New York Times, 1870-1880.

Texas, Jacksboro: Frontier Echo, 1877.

Army and Navy Journal (New York), 1848-1881.

Chronicles of Oklahoma (Oklahoma Historical Society, Oklahoma City), vol. 2 (1924), no. 1.

MUSEUM RECORDS

Cavalry Museum, Fort Riley, Kansas; Cavalry Museum, Fort Bliss, Texas; Fort Sill Museum, Fort Sill, Oklahoma; Kit Carson Museum, Taos, New Mexico; Lincoln Memorial, Springfield, Illinois.

BOOKS

Bancroft, Hubert H. History of Arizona and New Mexico (Albuquerque, New Mex., 1962)

Bancroft, Hubert H. History of California, vols. 4-7, 1840-1890 (San Francisco, 1886-1890)

Bearss, Edwin C. Decision in Mississippi (Jackson, Miss., 1962)

Bennett, James A. Forts and Forays (Albuquerque, New Mex., 1948)

Berthong, Donald J. The Southern Cheyennes (Norman, Okla., 1963)

Brackett, Albert G. History of the United States Cavalry (New York, 1865)

Brandes, Ray. Frontier Military Posts of Arizona (Globe, Ariz., 1960)

Brill, Charles J. Conquest of the Southern Plains (Oklahoma City, 1938)

Brooks, N.C. Complete History of the Mexican War (Philadelphia, 1849)

Carriker, Robert C. Fort Supply, Indian Territory (Norman, Okla., 1970)

Carson, Kit. Autobiography, ed. by Milo M. Quaife (Lincoln, Nebr., 1966)

Carter, Robert G. On the Border with Mackenzie (New York, 1961)

Centennial of the United States Military Academy at West Point, New York, 1802-1902 (Washington, D.C., 1904)

Chandler, Melbourne C. Of Gary Owen in Glory (Arlington, Va., 1960)

Clarke, Dwight L. Stephen Watts Kearny (Norman, Okla., 1961)

Connor, Seymour V. and Odie B. Falk. North America Divided: The Mexican War, 1846-1848 (New York, 1971)

The Conquest of Santa Fe, by a Captain of Volunteers. (Philadelphia, 1847)

Cooke, Philip St. George. The Conquest of New Mexico and California (Chicago, 1964)

Corle, Edwin. The Gila (New York, 1951)

Coy, Owen C. The Battle of San Pasqual (Sacramento, 1921)

Cullum, George W. Biographical Register of the Officers and Graduates of the U.S. Military Academy, 1802-1890 (3 vols., Boston, 1891)

Cutts, James M. The Conquest of California and New Mexico (Albuquerque, New Mex., 1965)

Downey, Fairfax. The Buffalo Soldiers (New York, 1969)

Emory, William H. Notes of a Military Reconnoissance from Fort Leavenworth to San Diego, California (Washington, D.C., 1848; the House Exec. Doc. 41 edition includes Cooke's report and A. R. Johnston's journal)

Estergreen, M. Morgan. Kit Carson (Norman, Okla., 1962)

Flipper, Henry O. Negro Frontiersman (El Paso, Tex., 1963)

Frazer, Robert W. Forts of the West (Norman, Okla., 1965)

Frost, Lawrence A. The Court-Martial of General George Armstrong Custer (Norman, Okla., 1968)

Glass, Edward L.N. History of the Tenth Cavalry, 1866-1921 (Tucson, Ariz., 1921)

Griffin, John S. A Doctor Comes to California . . . with Kearny's Dragoons (San Francisco, Calif., 1943)

Grinnell, George B. The Fighting Cheyennes (Norman Okla., 1956)

Grivas, Theodore. Military Governments in California (Glendale, Calif., 1963)

Guinn, J.M. Historical and Biographical Record of Los Angeles (Chicago, 1901)

Haley, J. Evetts. Fort Concho and the Texas Frontier (San Angelo, Tex., 1952)

Heitman, F.B. Historical Register and Dictionary of the United States Army (2 vols., Washington, D.C., 1903)

Herr, John K. Story of the U.S. Cavalry (Boston, 1953)

Heyman, Max L., Jr. Prudent Soldier: E. R. S. Canby (Glendale, Calif., 1959)

Hughes, John T. Doniphan's Expedition . . . Kearny's Expedition to California (Cincinnati, 1847)

Hunt, Aurora. Major General James H. Carleton (Glendale, Calif., 1958)

Lambert, Joseph I. One Hundred Years with the Second Cavalry (Topeka, Kas., 1939)

Leckie, William H. Military Conquest of the Southern Plains (Norman, Okla., 1963)

Leckie, William H. The Buffalo Soldiers (Norman, Okla., 1967)

Lowe, Percival G. Five Years a Dragoon (Kansas City, Mo., 1906)

MacCartney, Clarence E.N. Lincoln and His Generals (Philadelphia, 1925)

Merrill, James M. Spurs to Glory (Chicago, 1966)

Moody, Loring. A History of the Mexican War (Boston, 1848)

Nye, Wilbur S. Carbine and Lance: The Story of Old Fort Sill (Norman, Okla., 1942)

Porter, Valentine M. Stephen Watts Kearny and the Conquest of California (Los Angeles, 1911)

Pratt, Richard H. Battlefield and Classroom (New Haven, Conn., 1964)

Reavis, L.U. Life and Military Services of General William S. Harney (St. Louis, 1878)

Richardson, Rupert N. The Frontier of Northwest Texas (Glendale, Calif., 1963)

Rickey, Don, Jr. Forty Miles a Day on Beans and Hay (Norman, Okla., 1963)

Rister, Carl C. Fort Griffin on the Texas Frontier (Norman, Okla., 1956)

Rister, Carl C. The Southwestern Frontier (Cleveland, Ohio, 1928)

Rodenbough, Theophilus F. From Everglade to Cañon with the Second Dragoons (New York, 1875)

Rodenbough, T.F. and W. L. Haskin. The Army of the United States, 1789-1896 (New York, 1896)

Sedelmayr, Jacobo. Missionary, Frontiersman, Explorer in Arizona and Sonora . . . narratives, 1744-51, ed. by Peter M. Dunne (Tucson, Ariz., 1955)

Sheridan, Philip H. Record of Engagements with Hostile Indians within the Military Division of the Missouri, 1868-1882 (Chicago, 1882; reprinted Bellevue, Nebr., 1969)

Stewart, Edgar I.   Custer's Luck (Norman, Okla., 1955)

Taylor, Joe F.   Indian Campaigns on the Staked Plains, 1874-75 (Canyon, Tex., 1962)

Turner, Henry S.   The Original Journals of H. S. Turner with Kearny's Expedition (Norman, Okla., 1966)

Twitchell, Ralph E.   History of the Military Occupation of New Mexico (Denver, Colo., 1909)

Upton, Richard.   Fort Custer on the Big Horn, 1877-1898 (Glendale, Calif., 1973)

Van de Water, Frederic F.   Glory Hunter: a Life of General Custer (New York and Indianapolis, 1934)

Wallace, Ernest.   Ranald S. Mackenzie on the Texas Frontier (West Texas Museum Association, 1964)

War of the Rebellion: A Compilation of Official Records of the Union and Confederate Armies (Washington, D.C., 1880-1901) Series I, vols. 5, 9, 11, 13, 17, 22-24, 26, 30-34, 39, 41, 44, 45, 47-53; Series II, vols. 4-6; Series III, vols. 2, 4

Webb, Walter P.   The Texas Rangers (Austin, Tex., 1965)

Whisenhunt, D.W.   Fort Richardson, Texas (El Paso, Tex., 1968)

Whitman, Sidney E.   The Troopers (New York, 1962)

Willard, Julius T.   History of the Kansas State College of Agriculture and Applied Science (Manhattan, Kas., 1940). Contains a section entitled "History of the First Professor of Military Science"

Williams, Kenneth P.   Lincoln Finds a General: volume 5, Prelude to Chattanooga (New York, 1959)

Wilson, James G. and John Fiske (eds.)   Appleton's Cyclopedia of American Biography, vol. 2 (New York, 1888)

Woodward, Arthur.   Lances at San Pasqual (San Francisco, 1948)

Wormser, Richard E.   Yellowlegs: the Story of the United States Cavalry (Garden City, N.Y., 1966)

Index